My 11th-grade Bible teacher knew
His lively, compelling lectures he
of ideas for articulating, and living out, a robust faith. You're holding
his book in your hands. In *Tough Issues: True Hope*, Luke Davis tackles
20 moral challenges that confront—and often vex—Christians today.
Written for teens and adults alike, this wide-ranging resource will
orient you to the waterfront of ethical conundrums – none of which
is hypothetical anymore.

MATT SMETHURST
Managing editor, The Gospel Coalition
Author, *Before You Open Your Bible*

No one who knows Luke Davis, excellent teacher and thoughtful
author, will doubt the quality of his work or its relevance. Luke's commitment to critical thinking as a core value in the classroom comes
through in this work with clarity. His careful scholarship and commitment to biblical education in the classroom over his career have
prepared him for the task at hand. This work will provide a valuable
resource to teacher and student alike as they consider the ethical issues
of today. More importantly, this work provides the tools to develop a
framework for critical thought on issues yet to be considered.

THOMAS L. FOLEY
Executive Director, Christian Educators Outreach

In *Tough Issues, True Hope*, Luke Davis offers a road map to well-
informed opinions about the critical issues of the day. He invites
dialogue around matters that are sometimes muddled and often
avoided in the midst of the ethical chaos which marks our current
cultural moment. Peppered with anecdotes and soaked in Scripture,
the reader learns to think carefully and live wisely. And all along the
way, he makes room around the table for those who may not accept
the Bible as authoritative. This book is bound to trigger engaging
conversations about 'tough issues' that cry out for solid answers.

TONY GILES
Assistant Pastor, Cornerstone Presbyterian
Church, Franklin, Tennessee

Luke Davis has the incredible ability to engage his readers in productive thought and dialogue about issues that matter. I have observed that ability in his teaching, his professional presentations, and in his relationships with others. I think he is a practical philosopher. His book *Tough Issues, True Hope* addresses key issues of the day with thoughtful, engaging consideration that confront key issues with understanding and a strong foundation in Biblical truth.

MICKEY BOWDON
Lead Partner,
Bowdon Miller Shepherding Group

Rev. Luke Davis' book, *Tough Issues, True Hope*, is an invaluable resource for teachers, parents, youth leaders, and anyone involved in educating and discipling young people. The complex issues and conflicting messages of a secular, social media driven, and divisive culture make discernment of truth, beauty, and right from wrong extremely challenging. Rev. Davis effectively utilizes a conversational style, personal anecdotes, and biblical references to facilitate clarity and understanding about the 'tough' issues of our day. The what/so what/now what construct—including compelling questions at the end of each chapter—challenges readers to know what they believe and why they believe it, and act on their beliefs regarding these complex issues in their daily lives.

JIM MARSH
Head of School Emeritus, Westminster
Christian Academy, St. Louis, Missouri

LUKE H. DAVIS

TOUGH ISSUES

TRUE HOPE

A Concise Journey through Christian Ethics

CHRISTIAN
FOCUS

Copyright © Luke H. Davis 2020

paperback ISBN 978-1-5271-0520-1
epub ISBN 978-1-5271-0577-5
mobi ISBN 978-1-5271-0578-2

10 9 8 7 6 5 4 3 2 1

Published in 2020
by
Christian Focus Publications Ltd,
Geanies House, Fearn, Ross-shire,
IV20 1TW, Great Britain.

www.christianfocus.com

Cover design by
Tom Barnard

Printed and bound by
Bell & Bain

Contents

Dedicated to the Brotherhood,
with deepest thanks

Billy Blea
Sean Carrick
Phil Covington
Kal Dawson
David Hearne
Paige Slyman
Lester Stuckmeyer
Jimmy Wittkop

PREFACE
Why This Book Exists

I am a teacher.

I am a teacher at a Christian high school in the American Midwest.

I teach classes on Biblical Ethics.

And there have been plenty of books written on the subject of ethics, morality, right and wrong. They have been written by recognizable authors and people knowledgeable in Christian teaching and how to communicate an understanding of ethical details.

So why I am writing another book on this subject? Good question, and a question that I asked myself more than once through this project. But I think I can construct an answer.

It's a book I never thought I would write in a format I never thought I could effectively manage. I'm used to writing fiction, so this book felt at times like I just flew into Tokyo and now I have to get around without a map (or any knowledge of the Japanese language!). I was actually encouraged to make a go of this by my wife. Christi thought it would be a good idea to take my teaching experience and turn it into a resource. As usual, she displayed tremendous insight, and she ended up believing more in this project than I did at many junctures. But as I approached this opportunity (writers try to call daunting projects 'opportunities'), I wanted it to be distinct in several respects.

I wanted this book to have a specific approach to each topic. In almost every chapter, you'll see a certain layout designed to facilitate our understanding of any issue, be it technology, abortion, divorce, or immigration. We need to have a firm grasp about what the issue is, that is, how we should define it. But we also need to realize these things matter and touch our lives in specific ways. And, because one's faith should be about things that provoke personal action, I want us to consider practical steps we can take or ways we can be involved as we apply God's teaching about the good life. In short, we need to have intellectual understanding, passionate attachment, and practical application. To keep with this theme, each chapter will present the 'what', the 'so what', and the 'now what' of each topic.

I wanted this book to approach a specific question: If God has rescued His followers in Jesus by His grace—His undeserved love and favor shown through Christ's death and resurrection—through our faith, this places us in a new life. In short, we are reoriented toward a new goal – to please and honor God. This is our new life, what one might call the good life. In this good life, we are now free. We're not free to do whatever we desire if it goes against God's desire, but we are freed to pursue what will be noble, true, and edifying for us and others. This approach helps us, benefits others, and it directs others to God in an attractive way. Given this, I asked: How does our place in the good life transform our thinking on how we should live? If God rescues us to be His people, then how can our lives demonstrate our love for Him?

I also wanted this book to approach a specific reality. Worldwide, humanity is becoming less biblically literate than ever before. Therefore, I seek to employ two strategies. I don't think that it's wise or right to discount the Bible, especially as we need to train followers of Jesus in its content, teaching, and overarching story of redemption. That is why you will find biblical references and teaching throughout these pages. We simply have to train ourselves to take the Bible seriously and to seek God's truth in its pages. But we cannot engage with the larger world and automatically expect them to buy into the authority of the Bible. A number of people will dismiss Scripture out of hand; others might declare the Bible was a nice book for its time but not in more sophisticated days such as ours; still others may seek to dissect what they view as the Bible's deficiencies. I am not here to write a book on the defense of the Christian faith and Scripture (other people have done better work on that than I could), but I do think we need a strategy in hand for those who reject the Bible. In that spirit, I also want to consider some common-sense ways that God's path for right living aligns with how humans should function. Even if others don't accept the Bible as God's truth, logically God's revelation will be sensible living, and we don't necessarily have to quote a Bible verse to do that. In short, the Bible demonstrates God's road map for the good life, but then again, so do good old-fashioned critical thinking skills. Ideally, I'll put both on display.

I also want this book to have a specific pace. I want it to be conversational, anticipating the questions people may have on a topic, and to do so in a lively fashion. I also want it to be clear and lead readers (whom I anticipate would include high school students and young adults) to consider the details of each issue, why it should matter to us, and how we might practically work out edifying solutions in each area. Thus, almost all chapters will utilize a what/so-what/now-what format as a way of clarifying our understanding. But I also desire this book to be concise. I want to keep moving and not get too wordy. The chapters are short. That might be good for some and frustrating for others. Those who desire more detail could wonder why I don't turn over every rock for discussion. That's part of my conspiracy: I want this to be a resource that orients you to consider some robust yet introductory matters on each moral topic. That is, I want to take you a certain distance and then trust you to do more consideration, more research, more thought, more collaboration and discussion with others. Test what you read here and shake it out. I'm trying to get you started on that journey.

The good life of following Jesus is very demanding. But it is not a crushing list of do's and don'ts. Of course, there are boundaries and commands. But God's way is not a checklist, but a road of delight upon which He places His people. Before He entrusts Moses the prophet with the Ten Commandments to give to His people, God says, 'I am the Lord your God, who brought you out of the land of Egypt, out of the house of slavery' (Exod. 20:2). He is saying, 'I have rescued you because I love you, and I love you simply because I want to love you, and here is how you journey on under my loving care: By seeking my desires, not primarily because you have to, but because you want to.'

What are those territories we encounter along our journey on the good life? That road is straight ahead!

PART ONE
IDEAS MATTER

IT'S tempting to plunge right into some of the more vexing matters we think pass for moral issues. Don't worry: If you can't wait for topics such as murder, sexuality, the environment, and others, they'll come later (actually, there's nothing I can do to prevent you from skipping ahead, but I'd plead for your patience). But I think there's a critical component to living the good life well that I don't want to overlook.

Ideas matter. The expression of your ideas matters to God and to others. And the communication you receive from outside sources (and how you use those outside sources) matters also. And the ideas we form about people who come from different backgrounds—socially, economically, and ethnically—matter too.

The purpose of this section is to explore those ideas. How do we use our words to communicate what's in the recesses of our hearts? As we ingest the ideas of others, how do we critically and wisely use the sources by which we access the world outside ourselves? What does it mean to demonstrate a humane, friendly, and live-giving stance toward other people? What does God communicate to us so that we are fortified to answer these questions well?

Now you can dive in!

1

The Words We Use

WHAT do the following all have in common?

- On the day of the 2016 United States presidential election, the swell of online traffic bulged on Twitter amongst its 321 million registered users. Throughout the day until 10 p.m. ET, there were forty million election-related tweets posted on the social media site.[1]

- On the morning that I began writing this chapter, the Inclusive Language Guide of Colorado State University listed 'America', 'American', 'male', and 'female' as words to be avoided in usage. The university also listed 'war', 'cake walk', 'hold down the fort', and 'starving' as other expressions deemed as non-inclusive.[2]

- Social and political commentator Dave Rubin repeatedly receives heavy praise for his *Rubin Report* show, which features extended sit-down conversations with a variety of personalities such as television host Larry King, neuro-

---

1. https://www.nytimes.com/2016/11/09/technology/for-election-day-chatter-twitter-ruled-social-media.html

2. https://www.campusreform.org/?ID=13460

scientist and atheist Sam Harris, political commentators Ben Shapiro and Thomas Sowell, and university professor Jordan Peterson. Of special note are Rubin's generous listening skills, his open-mindedness, and lack of agendas or 'gotcha' questions.[3]

● Citizens of Hong Kong, in response to criminal and anti-extradition bills which they believe could leave them at the mercy of the Chinese government, turn out in throngs of anywhere from half a million to two million people in June 2019 to register their anger with the proposition.[4]

The answer is 'They all use words.'

The way we communicate ideas is a foundational part of human nature. One of the most noted milestones for children is their first word. How we utilize language, arrange thoughts, and express our inmost being taps into our great passions of life. In addition, the freedom to express oneself—whether individually or in more socially extensive ways like freedom of the media or the liberty to hold protests—is viewed by many as the primary freedom of all people (though I would argue the right to life outranks it, but that comes later in this volume). A significant number of people will base the quality of their nation, and their government, on the metric of free speech.

The Economist published its 'Democracy Index' a couple of years back, in which it mentioned that the 'quality of democracy in any country may in large part be gauged by the degree to which freedom of speech prevails. Societies that do not tolerate

---

3. https://www.thedailybeast.com/free-speech-true-believer-dave-rubin-the-top-talker-of-the-intellectual-dark-web-doesnt-want-to-talk-about-his-own-ideas

4. https://www.hongkongfp.com/2019/07/05/hong-kong-extradition-bill-battle-continues-protests-planned-weekend/

dissent, heresy, and the questioning of conventional wisdom cannot be "full democracies".[5] I think it is true that there's a solid link between free speech and the quality of government, and that should be a concern for all citizens. But that is not what brings us to this chapter.

We are asking, what are the components of the *good life* that Jesus calls us to live? And while free speech is a wonderful right (and I definitely don't want to lose mine!), the issue is not how do we use Jesus' teaching to defend our rights of expression. We have to ask how we should use our words.

With that in mind, let's start.

'What?': Speech, Free and Otherwise

The drama of human history is only a few sentences old before we discover that someone is *talking.* Genesis 1 exhibits the importance of the expressed word, showing us that the world is constructed *by the speech of God.* The New Testament underscores this when one writer shares that 'the universe was created by the word of God' (Heb. 11:3), or more literally, *the ages were formed by the speech of God.* Verbal communication is the reason why things exist. God spoke, and the elements of the world began whizzing into formation. He used imperatives, or commands, which shows that everything good in the world—including your existence—is an expression of His intention and purpose.

Obviously, God is not the only being equipped for speech. He invests His human creation with that gift, and people manifest this ability in stunning ways. They might celebrate God's goodness, as Adam shows his elation when God creates Eve for him as a wife (Gen. 2:23). People can declare God's worth, as Solomon did at the dedication of the Jerusalem Temple, praying

---

5. http://pages.eiu.com/rs/753-RIQ-438/images/Democracy_Index_2017.pdf

aloud that 'there is no God like you in heaven above or on earth beneath' (1 Kings 8:23). Prophets such as Nathan, Elijah, Elisha, Isaiah, Jeremiah, and others spoke God's messages of mercy and judgment to His people. And Jesus Himself—known for tangible actions like miracles and healings—spent much of His ministry on earth teaching people about God's kingdom and using parables as stories to exemplify what that journey was like.

Also, verbal proclamation is the primary vehicle by which people have been moved to action over the years. Biblical preaching is God's non-negotiable activity by which people hear the truth of salvation in Christ and growth in divine grace. The Apostle Paul makes this clear to his protégé Timothy when he commands him to 'preach the word; be ready in season and out of season; reprove, rebuke, and exhort, with complete patience and teaching' (2 Tim. 4:2). Working from Scripture, which is 'living and active, sharper than any two-edged sword' (Heb. 4:12), followers of Jesus can have confidence that they will receive truth that is essential for godly living.

Speech also moves people by the power of words and compels others to remembrance and action. This can be demonstrated by memorable speeches and addresses down through time. Historic examples include Winston Churchill's 'We Shall Fight on the Beaches' speech to Parliament in 1940 ('we shall never surrender'); the inaugural address of John F. Kennedy; Martin Luther King's electrifying 'I Have a Dream' speech during the March on Washington; Ronald Reagan's urging in Berlin to 'tear down this wall'; Abraham Lincoln's 'Gettysburg Address'; and Sojourner Truth's passionate 'Aren't I a Woman?' speech in 1851. Even fictional speeches like King Henry's stirring address to the English troops on St Crispin's Day in Shakespeare's *Henry V* coin enduring phrases ('band of brothers') and inspire future generations.

The point is that verbal communication is a gift from God. The ability and hunger to express oneself, to utter thoughts and opinions, to tell stories and publish poems (because some of us, like me, do better at writing things out than speaking them) is a profound facet of being made in God's image.

'So What?': Speech Spoiled

Aside from the potential to edify and uplift others, our words also carry with them great power to divide and destroy. Note what the Apostle James says in the third chapter of his epistle:

> Look at the ships also: though they are so large and are driven by strong winds, they are guided by a very small rudder wherever the will of the pilot directs. So also the tongue is a small member, yet it boasts of great things. How great a forest is set ablaze by such a small fire! And the tongue is a fire, a world of unrighteousness. The tongue is set among our members, staining the whole body, setting on fire the entire course of life, and set on fire by hell. For every kind of beast and bird, of reptile and sea creature, can be tamed and has been tamed by mankind, but no human being can tame the tongue. It is a restless evil, full of deadly poison. With it we bless our Lord and Father, and with it we curse people who are made in the likeness of God. From the same mouth come blessing and cursing. My brothers, these things ought not to be so (James 3:4-10).[6]

Our ability to speak can create more impact that goes well beyond the (relatively) small size of our tongue (and vocal cords). In seven verses, James compares our power of speech to (a) an uncontrollable rudder on a ship, (b) a fire, (c) a poisonous stain, (d) an instrument of hell, and (e) untamable. In short,

---

6. While this is just taken from James 3:4-10, the whole chapter, and indeed the entire epistle, is worth reading.

our words—which can bless and encourage—also have the ability to (a) get us and others off course from where we should go, (b) savage and tear down people, (c) smear, tarnish and toxify reputations, (d) do Satan's bidding, and (e) refuse to get under control. James ends this with an exhortation that the contradictory, hypocritical action of blessing and cursing should not come from people transformed by the good news of Jesus.

Aside from the difficulty of bringing one's own speech under control, we live in a worldwide environment marked by a sharp decrease in civility, tact, and kindness. In spite of the best efforts of many to make decency and empathy more apparent, social media and online blogs open up too many opportunities for people to load up their untamable selves to spew controversial and harmful opinions.

There also exists much confusion about where different sorts of communication might be welcome. In a number of American universities and colleges, for example, the designation of 'free speech zones' and 'safe spaces' has literally carved out places where discussion of controversial and disturbing issues might be either welcome or barred.[7] For places that ideally should be citadels of discussion and generous debate, it is difficult to see how this artificial sectioning can nurture the growth of emerging adults rather than imprison them in deepening immaturity.

Recently, this anxiety has erupted in specific protests. Bret Weinstein, an evolutionary biology professor at Evergreen State College in Washington, found himself at the center of a verbal storm in 2017. Evergreen State had for years observed a tradition known as a Day of Absence, in which students and faculty of minority races would stay away from campus for the day. This was not to bar them or discriminate against them,

---

7. https://thebestschools.org/magazine/speech-codes-and-safe-spaces/

but to highlight (by their absence) how critical the minorities' contributions had been throughout history. In 2017, a collection of students and professors challenged this and wanted to flip the tradition, barring white students and faculty from campus for the day. Weinstein firmly spoke out against the 'flip',[8] earning him an astounding level of anger from many students, who sought to bar him from campus and also took over the college library and shouted down anyone who disagreed with their conclusions.[9] This hardly seems to be a generous arrangement for the exchange of ideas with deliberation and thoughtfulness.

Of course, this is not limited to those of more 'progressive' views. Traditionalists and conservatives can exhibit like traits, unloading vile statements and personal attacks on others, even those within their tribes.[10] Such actions have much to do with blurting out whatever is on one's tongue and less than they might think about exhibiting the spirit of Jesus Christ.

'Now What?': Speech Redeemed

As I referenced before, I think the idea of free speech is a good one, and it's a cornerstone of a freer society. I live in the United States, where I am more than happy that the First Amendment of our Constitution specifically declares that 'Congress shall make no law respecting an establishment of religion, or prohibiting the free exercise thereof; *or abridging the freedom of speech, or of the press, or of the right of the people peacefully to assemble,*

---

8. https://www.nytimes.com/2017/06/16/us/evergreen-state-protests.html

9. https://www.washingtontimes.com/news/2017/may/25/evergreen-state-students-demand-professor-resign-f/

10. Witness leaders such as university presidents (https://www.christianpost.com/news/evangelical-divide-explodes-over-migrant-children-after-jerry-falwell-jr-slams-russell-moore.html) and pastors (https://friendlyatheist.patheos.com/2019/06/29/robert-jeffress-democrats-claiming-to-be-christian-dont-worship-the-true-god/).

and to petition the Government for a redress of grievances.'[11] This makes for an existence where we (in principle) can have a great deal of latitude of expression, in a spirit of tolerance where we do not have to agree with someone else, yet that other person would have the right to say what they wish. A couple of truths need to be stated as we practically work this out.

One matter is for everyone, whether Christian or not. If you subscribe to the political principle of free speech, it is not a gift given to you with limitations to others. Uncomfortable and disturbing words (providing they do not demonstrably incite violence) would be given a place in the world along with your own beliefs. For instance, members of the Westboro Baptist Church (which is more like a cult than a Christian community) in Topeka, Kansas, travel around the nation to protest both at events celebrating the achievements of homosexuals and at the funerals of American soldiers killed in action, claiming such deaths are God's judgment on America for tolerating homosexuality. Now I don't affirm homosexuality (as you can discover in a later chapter) and neither do I think military deaths display God's judgment in a discernible way. But we have to ask if we can just eliminate some verbiage from our surroundings simply because it is offensive. If you are a Christian, do you want an atheist to be silenced if he or she mocks the idea that Jesus is the Son of God? It's important to play fairly. Free speech protects unpopular speech.

There is another item to consider if you are a follower of Jesus. Whether or not you live in a nation that has free speech, the Bible never guarantees you have that right. God is more interested in your speech and your communication being *faithful* than *free*. For one reason: Not every Christian lives in a free society. A number of believers inhabit oppressive nations

---

11. *We the People: The Citizen and the Constitution* (Calabasas, CA: Center for Civic Education, 2009), p. 207.

like North Korea, China, Turkey, Vietnam and others, where they do not have the benefits of free expression but always are under the biblical directive to obey Christ with what they say. Another reason is that God gives us different parameters for judging the quality of our words:

(1) Is what I say true? That is, does it match with reality? The Apostle Paul urges Christians to emphasize 'whatever is true … honorable … just … pure … lovely …. commendable' (Phil. 4:8). As a follower of Jesus, you do not get to pop words out of your mouth indiscriminately without measuring them well. God is a God of truth. Everything Jesus spoke was truth, and everything the Holy Spirit reveals to Jesus' followers is true. So, if we are to imitate Jesus and grow in His nature, then our speech and communication should follow the same truthful trajectory.

(2) Is what I say helpful? As the Christians in ancient Thessalonica looked with anxiety toward the future, Paul reminded them of our mutual life in Christ, and then he says, 'Therefore, *encourage one another and build one another up,* just as you are doing' (1 Thess. 5:11, *my emphasis*). Rather than sucking the life out of someone, we should seek to strengthen them with what we say. This doesn't mean we can't ever criticize someone when it's called for. However, the goal of our communication should be pouring hope and healing into others by what we share. Are people lifted up when you are around them? Do people view you as an encourager?

One of my former college room-mates has spent a great deal of time as a public school principal in Alabama. One of Danny's greatest gifts is his strategic desire to mingle with students and seek out kids who might need encouragement. Whether it is a positive statement or a question of how they are doing that day or giving them a high-five hand slap with a smile, Danny knows how to take a student and empower them to lift up their head a little more. That is an intentional attitude which takes dedication and practice, and the more we seek to turn that spirit into habitual action, the more clearly we will communicate helpful, encouraging, strengthening hope.

(3) Is it necessary? Jesus counsels His disciples in Matthew 5:33-37 about taking oaths, such as in a court of law. Technically, He is speaking to this specific matter when He tells them 'Let what you say be simply "Yes" or "No"; anything more than this comes from evil.' But surely there is no problem with broadening this to a more general application here. Yes, we should tell nothing but the truth, but does that mean we should go into a mind-boggling amount of detail every time? This is especially important when people have told us information we should hold in confidence. If your friend Tyler is facing the divorce of his parents, he might let you know about his struggles but ask you to keep this matter private for now. Perhaps your other friend Maggie asks, 'What's going on with Tyler?' In that case, you don't need to give the details. You can say, 'Who can say?' or something innocuous like that. Or just shrug and say nothing. Or perhaps a ferocious argument breaks out near you, and it's clear no one is wanting constructive dialogue, so any engagement in the verbal struggle is fruitless. Have you thought that you can just walk away or disengage? You don't have to attend every fight that invites you in.

There are other questions to consider, but these should get you started on a road toward more thoughtful speech. If you live in a society where you can speak freely, be thankful. But remember also that your freedom of speech does not free you from the consequences of opening your mouth. People are free to disagree with you. They can push back against your ideas. That's good and healthy. It forces you to be more thoughtful about how true, helpful, and necessary your ideas might be. There's no reason to fear this, especially as a follower of

Jesus. We have His promise that if we are earnestly wanting to communicate truthfully to others, even if we are under the scrutiny and skepticism of others. His words to His disciples then must penetrate our hearts today when He exhorts us to 'not be anxious about how [we] should defend [ourselves] or what [we] should say, for the Holy Spirit will teach you in that very hour what you ought to say.' (Luke 12:11b-12)

For Your Consideration

- Why is it so important to communicate our ideas clearly and graciously?

- Note the implications of what James 3 reveals about our speech. In what areas of your speech do you struggle with exhibiting biblical faithfulness?

- If people's free speech should be protected as a right, what is our responsibility when we encounter hateful words, unpopular ideas, or statements that clearly could lead to physical violence?

2

Technology, Social Networks, and Faithful Living

IN Gregory Stock's *The Book of Questions,* he posits this question for discussion: 'Assume there were a technological breakthrough that would allow people to travel as easily and cheaply between continents as between nearby cities. Unfortunately, there would also be 100,000 deaths per year from the device. Would you try to prevent its use?' When I pose this query to my students, the consensus is they would never allow the device to see the light of day. Apparently, getting from St Louis to London in fifty minutes isn't worth the potential loss of human life. But Dr Stock comes back to this question later in his book when he notes 'In the mid 1800s, had you been able to look into the future and see that the automobile would cause five million fatalities in the next century, how would you have felt about this new device?'[1] Yes, that works out to 100,000 deaths per year from the automobile, and yet no one questions or pushes back against its existence, nor do people deny it's better to drive one's Honda to the movies rather than

---

1. I can't recommend Stock's book enough for conversation starters or personal growth. https://www.amazon.com/Book-Questions-Revised-Updated/dp/0761177310

walk or take a horse carriage a distance of ten miles (except for Amish communities, perhaps). All of this is to say that when we introduce new technology, there are some drawbacks that we must recognize alongside the benefits.

In a similar fashion, inhabiting a world without online social networks is well-nigh impossible. I could sooner imagine my father without a nose than a world without Facebook, YouTube, Twitter, Instagram, Pinterest, Snapchat, Whisper, and so on. Our world is hyperconnected and cyber-enmeshed, and it's unreasonable to think it will become less so.

Still, even though society has a given environment, our actions within it are not automatically good at best or neutral at worst. Social media and networking can be used for good or for evil. I don't think one can shout against the use of such platforms, nor can we expect to live 'off the grid' from any techno-reach. You can see this book is the result of technology—not the least because I wrote it on my laptop with Internet access—and when it's published, I fully expect to promote it on my Facebook and Twitter accounts. But the rapid speed of life brought on in our overly connected world means we have greater difficulty in slowing down and assessing if our experiences are good, noble, and true.

'What?': The Speed and Action of Technological Life

The Internet is not solely guilty of speeding up what was once a manageable human rate of existence, but it has certainly played a role in moving life velocity several Machs upward. The American architect and theorist Buckminster Fuller [1895-1983] coined the term 'knowledge doubling curve.' From his research, Fuller discerned that until the twentieth century, the amount of human knowledge in the world doubled nearly every century. At the end of the Second World War, the rate changed to where knowledge was doubling every twenty-five years. Now, well over a quarter-century after the first World Wide Web browser was released to the general public, human knowledge doubles every thirteen months. And IBM estimates that we could eventually hit a critical mass of knowledge doubling every *twelve hours!*[2]

This speed affects us in a variety of ways. First, our brains cannot process life at its warp speed. It is true that we can increase the processing speed of our brains, which are blessed with a reasonable amount of neurological plasticity. We can make new pathways, new connections, and increase the amount of neural circuits. Our brains can be highly adaptable organs.[3] However, we still have to make deliberate decisions about what we will pay attention to and what we need to dump by the side of the cyber-road. There is only so much information overload we can reasonably handle. A good analogy is your cable, satellite, or Internet television service. Whether you are a patron of Charter, Comcast, DirecTV, Dish Network, SlingTV, or YouTubeTV, you practically end up with a handful of channels that become your favorite; there is much of your product you don't (and can't) reasonably use.

Secondly, the speed of technological information makes it difficult to discern what information is true and what isn't. Granted, there is digital media that is deliberately satirical and makes no pretense of being legitimate news sites; examples include The Onion and the Babylon Bee. But when we get online and check out sites like CNN, Fox News, Bloomberg, *The Economist, The Guardian,* and others, we expect more light than heat.[4] Yet the speed of the news cycle means the competition to

---

2. http://www.industrytap.com/knowledge-doubling-every-12-months-soon-to-be-every-12-hours/3950. Keep in mind there are several fields where knowledge doubling varies from the general average. For example, atomic engineering doubles its knowledge every two years.

3. https://www.cognifit.com/science/cognitive-skills/processing-speed

4. Although you might not agree fully with the plotting of this chart, Market Watch made an attempt to show where different sites fall on a spectrum of

get ratings and website hits and to be the first person or group to break the story has intensified. This can lead to a lack of fact-checking and a story that is less than true or helpful.

Also, the speed of life can play havoc with one's spiritual journey. I am not disdaining the use of technology in the church (our church has song lyrics on the screens for our 9 a.m. service, after all!), but when we allow ourselves to be carried away by a hyperconnected lifestyle and are constantly wedded to our devices, the chances are we are not rooted enough to abide in Jesus so that we can grow in the grace He provides. The Christian heart and will is nurtured and fortified when one takes conscious, deliberate steps to walk at Jesus' pace and not try to get Him to adjust to ours. I love what the late Michael Yaconelli says about how this happens:

> Spiritual growth is not running faster ... Spiritual growth happens when we slow our activities down. If we want to meet Jesus, we can't do it on the run. If we want to stay on the road of faith, we have to hit the brakes, pull over to a rest area, and stop. Christianity is not about inviting Jesus to speed through life with us; it's about noticing Jesus sitting at the rest stop.[5]

'So What?': Technology and Life

I'm not asking any of us to go Amish and torch our computers and iPhones. I do think what's helpful is to take a sober look at how the connectedness of technology can be at once a benefit and a bane.

---

political bias and factual reporting. It's helpful for getting a wide-angle view of things, if nothing else. See https://www.marketwatch.com/story/how-biased-is-your-news-source-you-probably-wont-agree-with-this-chart-2018-02-28

5. From Yaconelli's book *Messy Spirituality: God's Annoying Love for Imperfect People*. I literally cannot praise this book too highly. It's simultaneously a passion-raiser and a soul-rescuer.

In a way, technology—and especially elements of social media—have made people more relationally linked than ever before. After I graduated from college in the early 1990s, we were still several years away from e-mail being a method of interpersonal discourse. If you wanted to connect with someone, you would have to either write them a letter or note and send it through the postal system, or you would call your friend for a chat. And by 'call' them I mean—in those days before everyone had a mobile phone—you would use a telephone wired in your home. I even remember the days before cordless phones when you would have to stand next to the phone when you talked because the cord connected the handset to the base unit of the phone; you couldn't go wandering off![6] Now I can open my laptop to Facebook and discover in two seconds that my college mate's oldest daughter is getting married. Celebrations are more instantaneous and replies flow quickly. I've found friends and acquaintances through social media that had been out of my life for some time and the relationships have come roaring back, and I've also been able to be more broadly connected with people at my work, church, and other places.

Technology also makes life more efficient. Just this week, my daughter and I were at a museum in southwest Missouri that had some vintage tractors and other equipment. There was an old Maytag wringer washing machine sitting in a corner and I showed Lindsay that people would use this to wash their clothes, cleaning them in the basin with the agitator and then squeezing it through the wringer above.[7] Needless to say, she

---

6. I can't believe I'm caving and using Wikipedia, but if you need to see what life was like back in the Dark Ages, read this: https://en.wikipedia.org/wiki/Telephone

7. I fully realize the irony of sending you to YouTube in a chapter that will offer some criticism of technology, but you can see an interesting demonstration of the Maytag here at https://www.youtube.com/watch?v=9BsDkGNxWOA

was glad washers and dryers have become less hands-on over the years!

Also, purchasing becomes more efficient. Last night, the St Louis Blues won the championship of the National Hockey League. Thanks to the Internet, our family doesn't have to drive twenty minutes to a shop to buy commemorative Blues champion shirts; we can order them online.

However, technology brings challenges to life beyond the increasing speed of our existence. For one, we can spend so much time with our noses buried in our phones or other devices that we become much more isolated and less human. More 'screen time' increasingly translates to less time sleeping (hence, less functional ability when awake) and less time spent talking face to face with others. I can affirm that many of my students struggle in this area, opting to send texts or scroll through their Instagram feeds, while the attempt to make eye contact with others becomes a Herculean effort. The overuse of social media is linked to a significant rise in depression and mood disorders amongst young people.[8] It seems as if withdrawing into oneself is the result of unrestrained access to social media and technology, making one question just how 'social' it is. The spike in online bullying, which has led to no small number of emotional breakdowns and suicides amongst adolescents, is another example of how technology can be used to divide rather than bring together.

Technology can also become more idolatrous, meaning we devote ourselves more to having it and accessing its benefits than anything else. And when that is taken from us, it reveals something about the nature of our hearts. How easy is it to let go of your device? I get that there are a number of technological

---

8. https://psychcentral.com/news/2018/11/11/too-much-screen-time-linked-to-anxiety-depression-in-young-children-and-teens/139931.html

advances that many of us can't live without (I do need a refrigerator to keep my milk and eggs fresh, of course), but are there items you can do without and be perfectly fine? And if you can't be fine without them—your iPhone, for example—isn't that somewhat revealing? And we have to beware of technology making life less realistic. Yes, it's nice to be more connected and more efficient, but we become more human and experience greater personal growth when we are able to put our devices away and just decompress, have a conversation over a cup of tea, take a walk outside among the trees or on a beach, and so forth. I think especially of how the life of faith progresses.

Yes, it would be easy to flip out a phone and get on a Bible app to follow along with Scripture readings in church. But the fact that that is easy is why I get worried. I worry about the subtle tendency to believe that because something is at my fingertips, then God's activity and answers will always be at my fingertips for easy access. And the life of biblically-minded, robust faith is not hyper-wired. We can't click a button and get an instant answer from the Holy Spirit. Sometimes we need to be content with some dry spiritual wastelands and struggles. Your life's purpose is not to 'click' with what's around you; your life's purpose is to follow Christ wherever He might lead you. And those areas will include stretches that batter you and don't give you easy answers, and nothing—not even your iPhone and access to Snapchat—will get you through that until Jesus is done teaching you what He wants to chisel into your heart.

'Now What?': Using It Well

It's hard to pull together a common-sense understanding and approach to technology and social media in less than three thousand words, but I think there are some practical considerations for us.

1. Utilize the blessing of technology wherever it exists. Where it helps you connect with others, celebrate that! We've discovered dozens of families on Facebook whose boys suffer from the same neuromuscular disorder that our Joshua has. We are able to encourage one another during hardships involving doctors, home health nursing organizations, durable medical equipment questions, and so on. It can be an incredibly life-giving array of moments to engage with others in need, and we're thankful for that.

2. Really consider the challenges that technology brings to your life. Ask yourself the following questions, and give honest answers. Are you addicted? Do you find yourself drifting out of conversations or reaching for your mobile phone to check if someone has texted or emailed you? Are you less able to manage tasks that demand much of your attention span? Are you becoming more irritated when something doesn't occur as quickly as you would wish? In short, really look at your techno-self and ask, 'What kind of person am I becoming?'

3. If you utilize social media to any extent, think about your usage. Consider the quality of your time spent. Are you giving an accurate picture of your life? Do you only advertise the high points and make people think everything is all strawberries and cream in your life? Or perhaps you are using your online platform to vent high drama about your struggles when the wise decision would be to not draw so much attention to yourself.

4. Think deeply about what responsible use looks like. In the Bible, there was great value in fasting from food during particular times for personal and spiritual focus. Perhaps there is great wisdom in strategic techno-fasting. When you

are with friends, put the mobile phone away and really open up the conversations. Get outside and leave your phones and laptops behind. I know of several people who intentionally don't check their Twitter, Instagram, or Snapchat for lengthy periods of time, whether it be for a brief weekend or an extended vacation. Or, if you do land on social media, target how you use your time. Instead of scrolling indiscriminately through the online feed, think of three or four of your good contacts or friends and check out their pages. Check in with them and let them know you're thinking about them. Maybe pray for them (in your head, that is … don't post the prayer online; it's weird). And then get off the site. Discipline will make for leaner, more strategic times online that will open moments for you to enjoy elsewhere.

These strategies may not fall into place at once. You might find some come more easily than others. But ideally, you will find that wise decisions of how you spend your online life will help you flourish in the good life that God calls to you enjoy.

For Your Consideration

- Imagine a person who lived in your community fifty years ago who has been transported to today. What might be some things they would notice—both positive and negative—about technology and the speed of life today? What about a person who lived a hundred years ago?

- Trying to match the fast pace of life might convince us that we can pace ourselves better than we are really capable. How might your 'life speed' cause problems for you intellectually, relationally, and spiritually?

- How social does social media make you? What are the benefits of being part of social media platforms and what might be some drawbacks?

- In calling us to 'the good life', Jesus beckons us to live holy lives that are pleasing to Him. How can you use technology in a way that honors Christ?

3

Diversity and Unity

A NUMBER of years ago, two separate pizza orders were bunched together at a Domino's Pizza shop in Charlottesville, Virginia. The delivery driver assigned to both orders took a quick look at a wall map in the back of the building to see where he would be going. The first delivery (based on the time the order was placed) was to be taken into a poorer section of the city; the second was placed from a house in a wealthier subdivision.

This set off a rumbling of wonder in the mind of the delivery person. *Perhaps,* he thought, *I could drop off the second order first! That's bound to be either a university professor or a well-to-do attorney. Likely I'll get a better gratuity than I will at the other place, especially if I get there in record time.* Back and forth, this man racked his mind trying to justify reversing the orders for delivery. But grudgingly, in the end he made up his mind to go to the poorer section of town first.

The light evening breeze cut through the summer humidity as the driver pulled up to a house whose paint job had seen better days. Hobbling down the steps of the front porch came an older man, dark as coal, fishing into his pocket and licking his lips. 'Thank you, young man,' he said as he thrust fifteen dollars into the driver's hand in exchange for a medium sausage pizza that cost just less than twelve dollars.

'Let me get you some change,' the driver dutifully replied. 'Nah, nah,' the old man waved him off. 'Been looking forward to this, and I'm glad to pay you for it. Life is short … don't have much time to be generous, so there you go.'

Humbled, the driver promptly went to the next house. Yes, it was the domicile of a prominent Charlottesville attorney. An attorney who pressed bills and coins into the hand of the driver for the exact amount. No gratuity.

In the delivery drivers' world, that's called 'getting stiffed.'

The driver experienced generosity from one who was poorer and Black, and received nothing from the wealthy Caucasian.

All the way back to the store, the driver confessed his discriminatory attitude to God. He'd learned a lesson that needed to be pressed into his heart, one he still remembers today. I know this, because *I* was that driver.

'What?': Defining Our Attitudes

Everyone thinks in terms of differences, of labels. We distinguish and prefer things all the time, and in many of our waking hours, there's nothing wrong with that. If you are eating out at a restaurant, you might narrow down your entrée choices to a French dip sandwich or an order of fish and chips. You order the fish because that's what you prefer; in short, you <u>discriminated</u>. That is, you chose because you preferred something over something else.

There are forms of discrimination, however, that can range from innocuous to less helpful to toxic levels. We have to ask ourselves, 'Why am I favoring one thing over another? Or one person or group over another?'

<u>Prejudice</u>: This occurs when you have an opinion about a member of another group based on your notions of that larger community, not primarily because you know the individual.

On occasion, we pre-judge because we *have* to make a snap decision. Airline safety agents do this all the time, for instance, on the lookout for terrorists. But very often, most of us exhibit the prejudice we may have because it's the easy way out. Sweeping generalizations might make for conversational fodder or memorable stand-up comedy, but it is unfair to paint every white, Black, Latino, Irish, Jew, or Arab with the same brush. The same goes for political party affiliations. Don't assume that because you see someone labeled as a Democrat, Republican, Labour, Tory, or otherwise that you can accurately speak about them.

Bigotry: Bigotry is crossing the line into even more poisonous areas. This goes beyond assuming someone is like the whole group to an intolerance of another person or group simply because they are different. Bigotry has reared its ugly head in places like Northern Ireland, where Catholics and Protestants tore the city of Belfast apart during the Troubles of the 1970s and 1980s. It makes its impact today in Nigeria, where Fulani tribesmen butcher Christians simply because they are not Muslim.[1] And there are Christians in the United States who— while speaking out against homosexuality as a sin—go beyond this and show no grace to homosexuals themselves with any amount of decency.

Ethno-racialism[2]: You might notice that each issue goes deeper in layers, like a set of Russian nesting dolls. Ethno-racialism occurs when one believes their ethnicity is superior to others which are—by their definition—inferior and even sub-

---

1. https://guardian.ng/news/suspected-fulani-herdsmen-others-kill-32-in-kaduna-sokoto/

2. In truth, I tend to veer away from the term 'racism', as race is a notoriously tricky concept to define. I have paired the idea with ethnicity to show that the bigotry can target a range of things having to do with someone's language, culture, and social ancestry.

human. The treatment of Blacks in the United States, through the slave trade and the chattel slavery system where slaves were viewed as the owners' property and an inferior community, gives ample evidence of ethno-racialism.[3] The Balkan crisis of the late 1980s and early 1990s exploded as a result of Serbia's desire to expel Muslims and Croats from the region of Bosnia to make that area 'more purely Serbian.'[4] And the longest-running and deepest example of ethno-racialism is the anti-Semitism against Jews worldwide, shown most tragically in the Nazi Holocaust during Adolf Hitler's rule in World War II Germany.

Ideally, you see the exhibition of unhealthy and sinful attitudes toward other people. How we relate to people who are 'different' from us (however one defines that) is critical. If we are serious about following Jesus, then we have to ask ourselves 'How does the way I treat other people reflect how I express my devotion to Christ?'

'So What?': The Diversity God Intends

Our Creator crafted our planet to be an art gallery of the highest level, and the rich diversity that reflects the nature of God is something to be celebrated, not suppressed. Read Genesis 1 and 2 and take in the vast swath of what God fashions. And then notice God's command: 'Be fruitful and multiply and fill the earth …' (Gen. 1:28). He wants a world of human vibrancy, and God doesn't take too kindly to that dream getting derailed. In Genesis 11, you have that escapade of earth-dwellers bunching

---

3. Professing Christians, sadly, have not been immune from these disgusting sentiments. One of the foremost Southern theologians of the nineteenth century wrote that blacks were 'a graceless, vagabondish set', a 'vile stream from the fens of Africa', and a 'morally inferior race' (R. L. Dabney in *A Defense of Virginia*).

4. https://www.independent.co.uk/news/world/the-bosnia-crisis-serbs-croats-and-muslims-who-hates-who-and-why-tony-barber-in-zagreb-traces-the-1539305.html

together, hunkering down in their one language and common, solitary culture, never wanting to spread out but rather building a tower to heaven. So what does God do? He *creates more diversity* and *brings about a wider range of languages and tribes.* God is saying, 'There are not enough meats in this cultural stew. Let's make a beautiful tapestry of what I've designed humanity to be!'

Throughout the Bible, we find that followers of Jesus will come from a variety of backgrounds, cultures, and skin tones. Psalm 117 calls for praise to come from 'all nations' and 'all peoples.' Jesus even states boldly that His spiritual family is the result of when we 'go and make disciples of all nations' (Matt. 28:19). Jesus Himself healed the sick and suffering beyond His Jewish tribe.[5] The early church in Acts contained believers of Jewish and Greek backgrounds, and the followers of Jesus there had to commit themselves to working through issues of ignorance, misunderstanding, and inaction.[6] The spiritually immature and seasoned godly people worshiped side by side, as did meat-eaters and vegetarians,[7] as did the wealthy and the poor, who were to be honored equally.[8] And Revelation 7:9 gives us a cross-section of Jesus' followers, an assembly representing 'every nation, from all tribes and peoples and languages.'

This brief overview of Scripture is designed to show that God intended His people to be anything but homogenous. Diversity is a characteristic at the core of those God draws to Himself. But

---

5. For example, the Canaanite woman in Matthew 15:21-28.

6. Note Acts 6:1-7, where Greek-speaking Christian widows were overlooked in favor of their Jewish Christian counterparts. To deal with this in an equitable fashion, the apostles had to appoint servants (some believe this is the origin of 'deacons') to oversee the food distribution to the widows.

7. Romans 14:1-3

8. James 2:1-7

it is not just Scripture that verifies this truth. A common-sense approach to life supports the authority of the Bible, as well.

'So What?': Diversity and Logical Sense

First of all, diversity and an embracing approach toward people of different backgrounds have a positive effect on the individual, whether one believes the Bible or not. If you spend all your time around people who look, act, and think like you, it doesn't stretch you as a human being. I know that when I sit down with a Black or Latino colleague and have a conversation about their experiences in our workplace or their childhood, a new world opens up to me. People who are different from me in various ways expand my understanding of the world around me. They also can expose weaknesses in my understanding of things.

Another solid reason for connecting with a diverse array of people is because this practice builds empathy for others. Sharing struggles, priorities, and convictions that might be particular to your ethnic makeup, your social or economic experience, or your upbringing will tend to give others a greater willingness to imagine what life is like in your shoes. And leaning into the stories of others is a great way for you to perceive how they operate or might react in a given moment.

A former teacher at my school ran a ministry in the city of St Louis that engaged many ethnic Bosnians (in fact, St Louis has the highest number of Bosnians outside of the nation of Bosnia!). This teacher is a Christian, while Bosnians tend to be Muslim. He obviously will not be converting to Islam, and he might not be converting many Muslims to the Christian faith. But through his outreach, he spoke to a number of Bosnians who were forced to flee the unrest and the 'ethnic cleansing' from the Serbs who desired to wipe them out. He understood their dreams for their community as well as their fears. He was better positioned to minister to them because he understood what they had gone through to get to this point.

A further area where diversity is highly helpful is in the workplace. An organization that commits itself to hiring people from a variety of backgrounds will often find that such a move strengthens the company itself. The variety of ideas coming from an array of employees from a myriad of backgrounds yields more perspectives to draw from. Approaches to problem solving and marketing aren't as one-sided, and this sort of collaboration can be helpful when expanding into new areas. Employees who see that a range of perspectives are tolerated and a mosaic of talent is encouraged are in turn emboldened to (a) continue working there and (b) recruit new talent to the business.

'Now What?': Responding to Injustice and Restoring Hope

It is one thing to identify an issue; it is another to offer a solution and put it into action. If all we do is talk about a diverse environment, or building fair and just systems, and we don't exert any energy toward implementations ... well, that's the equivalent of pointing out a broken bone and neglecting to cast the fracture.

Admittedly, there's a tidal wave of ideas for how to construct a more diverse society, to build increasingly varied institutions, and how to right any wrongs that have been done to people groups due to bigotry or ethno-racialism. Some proponents of ethnic diversity advocate for reparations, financial payments for wrongs done to people groups in years past. Some Blacks have made the case for reparations to families of former slaves in the American South; how those payments would be made and by whom is a matter of debate.

Others believe reparations are not the most constructive measure, but they do see alternative means for justice. It is true, of course, that other nations have implemented such payments to redress horrific wrongs of the past. In the years that followed the Second World War, for example, Germany made financial payments to the nation of Israel and Jewish survivors of the Holocaust. This action, of course, did not bring back the massacred Jews who had been butchered by the Nazis, but Germany believed it should do what was in its power to do for the justice it could provide.

While agreement on the reparations issue might be difficult to reach, there are more local ways we can seek justice.[9] For example, here in St Louis, Missouri, one of the injustice eyesores of our municipality is the Medium Security Institution, known as the City Workhouse. The cramped quarters hold 550 people, many of whom are awaiting trial for a variety of alleged offenses. Yes, there are some violent criminals who need to be imprisoned without bail; however, the majority of the incarcerated are being held without bail for misdemeanors or probation violations, hardly dangerous actions. Unsanitary conditions[10] and threats on safety have been longstanding occurrences; in truth, many of those jailed can't afford bail for minor issues. And the group that is disproportionately affected by this are lower-income Blacks. Do you see the injustice evident there? Surely either closing the Workhouse or working out a solution to reduce the population thereof is a start?

Ultimately, issues of ethnicity, diversity, and justice need to be fleshed out at the individual level, because the attitude and stance one takes into the world around them will dictate their

---

9. Note: I define 'justice' as 'the act or process of giving or receiving what one deserves in a given situation.'

10. Like mold, rat, and insect infestations. For the whole story, see https://www.stltoday.com/news/local/crime-and-courts/efforts-grow-to-close-unspeakably-hellish-st-louis-workhouse/article_23d869b2-62b5-59e9-9f99-9dcc8cc74fca.html

response or lack thereof to injustice and the participation in a vibrant mosaic of humanity. If you have children, you need to encourage them to pursue friendships and connections with people who are outside their usual ethnic, social, and economic orbit. Really filter through how you go about your day and ask yourself, 'Are there people I tend to avoid? Why? Are there others who are different from me where, if a conversation is going on, I tend to speak and make my point but never listen to them? Do I look for those who are on the margins of life, who are excluded, who are the targets of injustice? What do I need to do to be part of a solution there?'

Obviously, the world is full of ideas well beyond these. My point is not to say there is one path for success laid out. Different people will disagree on the methods to foster diversity or combat injustice. But what I believe should be the top concern is this: Find a practical way, in the setting in which God has placed you, to make a difference. You might not change the world, but you can transform a portion of it. And even though we cannot eradicate the wrongs of history, we can be part of bringing in God's colorful dream for His world in the present and the future.

For Your Consideration

- How would you explain the distinction between bigotry and ethno-racialism in your own words? Where do you see evidence of these toxic attitudes in the communities around you?

- How would you go about convincing someone that bigoted and racialist attitudes and speech are wrong? How do you convince them that respect and honor toward all people make for a better life? What if this person doesn't accept the authority of the Bible or believe in the existence of God?

- If you haven't been a target of bigotry or ethno-racialism, practice some empathy right now. Imagine being on the receiving end of that type of prejudice. How might you respond, and how might you want others to advocate on your behalf?

- If you have been a recipient of bigotry or ethno-racialism, how did that experience affect you? What support did you need from others as you faced those moments?

PART TWO
LIFE MATTERS

WITHOUT a doubt, issues that touch on the dignity of and right to life get a lot of traction. People will have passionate opinions on matters such as capital punishment, abortion, suicide, and bio-engineering. This is understandable. No matter what our differences, one reality that unites us is that we are alive. And the possession of life is critical to navigating the good life. Let's be truthful: You cannot follow God's prescription for living if you possess neither breath nor bloodstream.

There is a logical pathway to travel for us to understand these issues. We will consider, in turn,

- What is the purpose of life? ('The Meaning of Life')

- What happens when life is unjustly taken? ('Murder and Capital Punishment')

- What about at the start of life? ('Abortion')

- What about life's sunset and matters of euthanasia? ('End-of-Life Decisions')

- What about afflictions that make people want to end their lives? ('Despair and Suicide')

- What about the living who experience severe limitations? ('Disabilities & Dignity')

- What should we think of those who push the borders of life? ('Bioethics')

Life is foundational to following in the way of Jesus. As we consider some heavy topics in the chapters ahead, may Jesus help us to faithfully approach the life He gives us.

4
The Meaning of Life

[NOTE: For this chapter only, I am invoking executive privilege and suspending the usual what, so-what, now-what format. Just this once.]

ONE Friday evening in 2009, when our daughter was eight years old, she spent the night at a friend's house out in a rustic area of the county. She and her friend Ellie were following the dog out into the woods for a brief walk before dinner. Convinced that Rosie the dog knew where she was going, they blindly trudged along until their growling bellies and the darkening sky told them they needed to be back at the house. But when they looked around, the house was nowhere to be seen. For nearly thirty minutes, Lindsay and Ellie desperately wandered around and only made their situation worse. Only the alert tracking abilities of Ellie's father saved them from spending a cold and brutal night in the woods (and from the police helicopter providing a sensational story for the ten o'clock news)!

There are discussions that end up that way, where we jump into an argument forgetting that it's not only *what* we discuss that matters, but *why* we do so that is of critical importance. Otherwise, we can have some significant adventures in missing the point and find—like Lindsay and Ellie—we're a long way from the location where we ought to be.

To begin any discussion of the sacredness of human life with the nosedive into the issue of murder, manslaughter, or general homicide is to commit oneself to this adventure in missing the point, however well-intentioned one's arguments may be. Such talks about the death penalty, abortion, end-of-life issues and other matters can be both polarizing and passionate. As energetic as these talks can get, we first have to engage deeper interrogations. We have to pose questions like, 'Why is life worth defending?' which still doesn't get at the core of the matter. Perhaps 'Why is life worth living?' is even better, but it still begs the question. 'What or who makes life worth living?' gives us sharper focus.

That prior final question gets asked in places ranging from college philosophy classes in New Hampshire to a lunch conversation between friends in Belfast to the trembling pleas of a young lady in Toronto who has endured sexual assault at the hands of a family member. Far from a theoretical matter, the common good of the human race hinges on how we answer it. Specifics may vary, but the question of the meaning of life comes down to three categories:

(1) Life has meaning because mine is a life of impact due to others noticing my achievements. (**Excellence**)

(2) Life has meaning because I am here on earth as a capable human being and I am exhilarated by life's possibilities, whether I am noticed or not. (**Existence**)

(3) Life has meaning because I—whether I make a tangible impact or not, and whether I seem capable or not—am a unique, special part of a Design or Designer. (**Essence**)

The first argument—the one from excellence—is commendable because, after all, the idea of achievement is far superior to the concept of aiming low. The ancient Egyptian Pharaoh

Senusret III declared, 'Vigor is valiant, but cowardice is vile.' Charles Kettering said, 'High achievement always takes place in the framework of high expectation.' And Pope John Paul II is reputed to have said, 'Do not be afraid. Do not settle for mediocrity. Put out in the deep and let down your nets for a catch.'

The Bible positively connects the dignity of work and achievement in many places. The Apostle Paul implored his readers, 'Whatever you do, work heartily ... knowing that from the Lord you will receive the inheritance as your reward' (Col. 3:23-24). The nobility of faithful labor comes shining through in Proverbs 13:4 where we are told that '[t]he soul of the sluggard craves and gets nothing, while the soul of the diligent is richly supplied.'

However, there is a firm distinction between doing one's best and being known for greatness. First of all, greatness can be snagged by dubious methods. While the case is rare, an A-level pupil can cheat to get excellent marks. Corporate accomplishments can be reached by practices devoid of any ethics. Standardized tests can measure how well you answer a math problem, but they don't measure creativity, honesty, or empathy. Or people might eventually want recognition without wanting to sacrifice for the prize. Consider the increasing slew of students in America's schools—public and private—that believe that the reception of a diploma is an automatic voucher to good fortune.

In addition, your known accomplishments aren't a good measuring stick of your self-worth or the meaning of life because of the simple reason that they will be forgotten. And it begs the question, 'What if I am never remembered? What then?' It does help to know that, as David McCulloch, Jn said so eloquently in his gone-viral-on-YouTube commencement address, you should 'climb the mountain, not to plant your flag, but to embrace the challenge, enjoy the air and behold the view. Climb it so you can see the world, not so the world can see you.'[1]

One would certainly believe, then, the answer comes in drawing the circle more widely, to say *Life has meaning because I am here on earth as a capable human being and I am exhilarated by life's possibilities, whether I am noticed or not.* This argument from <u>existence</u> may ring the bell more deeply at the core of our being because so much of what we do flies under the radar. We may say with Jean-Paul Sartre that 'man is nothing else than that which he makes of himself' as long as we make our peace that it might not be noticed. We are here, we exist, and we die, in our own capability and by our specific, unique talents. The Dutch humanist Erasmus was fond of saying, 'It is the chiefest point of happiness that a man is willing to be what he is.'

But is this what makes us special, what makes us unique, what makes life worth living or worth protecting? The moment we define humans by the sum of what they seem to be, we still have to ask the question 'What about the less endowed, the less talented, the less mobile, the intellectually compromised?' (and this is an issue we will come to in more detail momentarily).

Some time ago, I received news from an acquaintance whose infant son—stricken by a syndrome that affects his vision and his muscular development—died at less than two years of age. Even on little Brooks' short life journey, there were many issues. A neurologist told Jonathan and his wife Gabrielle that—while surgery was an option—they should expect their son to possibly be able to sit up, feed, look around, but not have much cognitive interaction, and then he would die after a year or two.

As a result of his disorder, Brooks was not able to recover, to do much more beyond sitting up, beyond the occasional stare

---

1. https://www.youtube.com/watch?v=_lfxYhtf8o4&t=6s

or smile. He was here for a season and now is gone. What if a treatment or cure for this syndrome is never found? Is it better that this child and others like him are never born? To those questions, I offer this corrective: If life is only worth living if the odds of suffering are greatly decreased, or if the odds of comfort and ability are higher, or if the person 'can contribute to society', then that betrays an attitude that we can make the call on people deemed less 'worthy.' And at what point do you draw *that* line?

The truth is that we are either designed on purpose—however flawed and limited our bodily abilities are—or we are not. Our essence is either that of people charged with and infused with dignity, or worthless piles of nothingness. There is no middle ground. I repeat: There. Is. No. Middle. Ground. Once you pluck human significance from the territory of being designed with dignity by a Source beyond us, everything is automatically up for grabs and you make your arguments with your feet planted in thin air.

So, how we answer the meaning-of-life question, bowing either to excellence, existence, or essence, will matter supremely. And before answering quickly or in a blithe fashion, consider this: Might the human race's default mode of living, as if there is something worth shooting for, give evidence that who we are matters, from the warmth of the womb to the cold of the tomb? It seems either to be that on one side or total despair on the other. How indeed could there be any middle ground?

For Your Consideration

- Why is it so critical to establish why life is valuable and precious before getting into particular issues like abortion, suicide, murder, and so on? Why do we miss the point if we don't consider this foundational matter?

- Without considering where the author ends up at the end of the chapter, think about the three views of excellence, existence, and essence. As you think about how you live each day, which view of the value of life do you tend to exhibit to others?

- The author makes this point near the end of the chapter: 'Our essence is either of people charged with and infused with dignity, or worthless piles of nothingness. There is no middle ground. I repeat: There. Is. No. Middle Ground. Once you pluck human significance from the territory of being designed with dignity by a Source beyond us, everything is automatically up for grabs and you make your arguments with your feet planted in thin air.' To what extent do you agree with this idea? Do you think there is a 'middle ground'? How do atheists, for example, build a case for human dignity without receiving our value from God? How credible is this, and why do you say that?

5

Murder and Capital Punishment

IN July 2009, a twenty-five-year-old man burst through an open window in a suburban Seattle house, attacking two women inside with savage abandon. Assaulting and torturing the ladies, he promised to spare their lives if they would comply with his demands. Instead, he stabbed one of them to death while the other barely managed to escape. At his trial, the killer defiantly roared that 'God told me' to kill the two women while family members of the victim wept nearby.

Charlottesville, Virginia, endured a different kind of horror in May 2005. A local doctor at the university medical center was arrested after an eleven-week investigation into child abuse allegations. The physician had attempted to burn his own three-month-old daughter with a hair dryer and drown her through forced water intoxication. Thankfully, the little girl survived and ended up with her mother instead, but the emotional scars run deep.

And in October 1986, a high school senior kissed his girlfriend goodnight after a midweek date. Driving home over the rural central Maryland countryside, he whisked over a two-lane highway, hoping to get home before midnight. He would never reach his destination, as a drunk driver coming from the other direction crossed into his lane, slamming head-on and snuffing out a promising life.

Murder. Attempted murder. Involuntary manslaughter. The abject sadness of these assaults on human life can and should leave us shaken. And I don't share these as random news occurrences. The murdered Seattle woman was the sister of my colleague and friend Jim. The doctor who tried to kill his daughter had overseen my son's hospitalization for respiratory infection just seventeen months before. And the young man killed by the intoxicated motorist was dating a good high school friend of mine.

These stories can and do hit home. Perhaps some of us can recount sobering accounts of which we are all too painfully aware. The taking of innocent human life is especially devastating because of the robbery of the gift of existence, a settled matter known as the *inalienable right to life*. Throughout the world, violence rears its ugly head in actions that cheapen humanity and show a disdain for personal value and worth. We've already looked at the meaning of life as a foundational principle. What happens when that is short-circuited in such a brutal fashion?

'What?': The Right to Life

Biblically, we find that God is the author of life, creating living creatures of the animal kingdom and—when fashioning the first human—breathing into him the breath of life. One of the first descriptions of a human being is 'the man became a living creature' (Gen. 2:7). When the first homicide occurs in Cain's killing of his brother Abel, God confronts the perpetrator and holds him accountable (Gen. 4:1-16). Later, when murder, mayhem, and rebellion over-run the human race, God bluntly declares *He is sorry that He created humans!* (Gen. 6:6).[1] Further along, God speaks to Noah, a man who

---

1. This might be the low point of human history. When God says that, it's pretty bad.

has survived a traumatic flood with his family[2] and He states, 'Whoever sheds the blood of man, by man shall his blood be shed, for God made man in his own image' (Gen. 9:6). We reflect God's attributes and we represent Him on earth; to violate this wonder is to attack God Himself. All this precedes the commandment, 'You shall not murder' (Exod. 20:13). Even Jesus—whom some people try to reduce to a nice teacher who made life more simple—makes the commandment *more difficult to follow*. In the event known as the Sermon on the Mount, Jesus presses the point that rage and anger are serious matters as unjust killing would be, for we must beware of murderous *attitudes*, which can lead to the murderous *actions* we must rightly hate.[3]

Not only do we find the value of human life presented in the Bible, the voices of human history uphold this principle as well. The English philosopher John Locke tenaciously held to a fundamental doctrine of the right to life. Within the fabric of human nature is the need to preserve the human race itself. What serves that intent, Locke reasoned, is an environment in which people have both a natural right and a complete duty to defend their own lives.[4] The American Declaration of Independence lists our 'inalienable rights'[5] as 'life, liberty, and the pursuit of happiness.' In 2007, Pope Benedict XVI addressed an assembly in Vatican City with the reminder that 'life is the first good received from God and is fundamental to all others; to guarantee the right to life for all and in an equal

---

2. Read Genesis chapters 6 through 9 for the entire captivating story.

3. Matthew 5:21-26

4. http://www.crf-usa.org/foundations-of-our-constitution/natural-rights.html

5. That is, freedoms that cannot be taken away from or given away by the possessor of those blessings.

manner for all *is the duty upon which the future of humanity depends.*'[6]

'What?': The Taking of Life

Homicide (the killing of a human being) is horrific, but not all manners of death should be considered equal.

Murder is the intentional taking of innocent human life with premeditation, strategy, and malice. In short, that involves thought, planning, and hatred. Murderers (if we apply police detective lexicons) utilize motive, means, and opportunity to snuff out the unsuspecting lives of their victims in cold blood. Murder occurs when the perpetrator has a desire or felt reason to kill (motive), the weapon or ability with which to kill (means), and the chance to carry out this horrific opportunity All of this is done in full presence of mind and reasonable calculation.

Voluntary manslaughter is slightly different than murder, although no less tragic. The desire to kill still exists; what is significantly heightened is the sense of provocation, the edge that causes someone to lose self-control and act rashly, suddenly, in the heat of the moment. Some have pointed to Exodus 2 as an example of this. Moses is walking through a work site and sees one of his fellow Hebrews beaten savagely by an Egyptian slave master. In a fury, he strikes down the Egyptian, kills him, and buries him in the sand. When news of his action runs through the greater community, Moses hightails it out of town before the king of Egypt can lay even a finger of vengeance upon him.[7]

---

6. http://w2.vatican.va/content/benedict-xvi/en/speeches/2007/february/documents/hf_ben-xvi_spe_20070224_academy-life.html (emphasis mine)

7. For the wider context in this story of what God is doing to rescue His people, read all of Exodus 1 and 2. Some scholars have maintained that Moses is guilty of murder, not manslaughter, but the details of the text don't give us any wiggle room to make that stick.

Involuntary manslaughter strips away a couple more pro-visions. There is no intent to kill, and neither does the killer employ premeditation nor is provoked to act. The core issue at the heart of this is irresponsibility or negligence. The previous account where the drunk driver killed the boyfriend of my friend Janet is such an example. The intoxicated motorist didn't intend to do what he did, but he was fatally irresponsible. All that was required was that he either not get drunk or find someone else to drive him home. Sadly, he did neither.

There are other categories of death which are accidental in nature, but for the purposes of this chapter, we will leave those to the side.[8]

'So What?': The Principle of Accountability

Part of God's post-flood conversation with Noah involved how society should function so that injustice might not overwhelm it to the degree as before. God's 'Whoever sheds the blood of man ...' statement from Genesis 9 is expanded in Exodus 21:23-25. There God maintains that 'if there is harm, you shall pay life for life, eye for eye, tooth for tooth, hand for hand, foot for foot, burn for burn, wound for wound, stripe for stripe.' This statement, called the *Lex Talionis*,[9] sets forth the guiding principle that the punishment must fit the crime – to seek justice, not revenge. This is a very demanding principle, but in truth it can be a very *undetailed principle*, because the exact manner in how one applies it can be particular to one's circumstances and culture. The one certain piece we can draw from that puzzle is

---

8. Witness the biblical situation (which hopefully remained hypothetical) in Deuteronomy 19, where God—as He implements the system of the cities of refuge for the Israelites' new homeland in Canaan—gives the example of two men supposedly chopping wood when an axe handle from one man's tool flies off and fatally strikes the other.

9. Meaning the 'law of retaliation'.

that the death penalty would be reserved for the worst and most heinous crimes, like murder. In implementing this allowance for His people at the time, God undeniably had two purposes in mind, preserving the dignity and worth of human beings, while also providing an outlet for justice so that society might function in a proper fashion.

It is true that during biblical times, the death penalty (a.k.a., 'capital punishment') was an accepted mode of accountability for a range of offenses. These included murder; kidnapping (Exod. 21:16); being a sorceress or commission of deviant, un-natural sexual practices (Exod. 21:18-19); adultery, incest, and homosexuality (Lev. 20:10-13); and being a false prophet (Deut. 13:1-5). It is also true that a number of societies today still maintain the death penalty as a legitimate mode of justice for what they judge to be especially heinous crimes. It is abundantly clear that Scripture demands accountability for sinful actions. It is just as true the Bible teaches the legitimacy of capital punish-ment. Still, some raise the question, *'Is capital punishment a requirement for a society to be truly just?'* The collision of these questions provokes strong debate amongst people of all faiths or no faith at all. The issue is prodded further in films such as *Dead Man Walking* and the Stephen King novel *The Green Mile.*

In my nation, the United States, thirty-one of the fifty states presently allow for the death penalty, even though some of those states haven't carried out an execution in years.[10] For each of these jurisdictions, the primary mode of execution is lethal injection.[11] In other nations that employ capital punishment, the methods range from the more humane to the greatly

---

10. http://www.pewresearch.org/fact-tank/2018/08/10/11-states-that-have-the-death-penalty-havent-used-it-in-more-than-a-decade/

11. The exact nature of the injection varies by jurisdiction. See https://deathpenaltyinfo.org/state-lethal-injection

barbaric. As one might expect, there is no commonly agreed understanding of what method should be used, let alone for what crimes.

Both critics and supporters of the death penalty employ an array of reasons they believe they are on the correct side of this issue. My concern is not to drive you toward one side or another, mainly because I believe this is a matter where people can agree to disagree without being disagreeable. I simply want to expand your understanding about what others believe and then return to some final important truths to which everyone should agree.

Those who are against capital punishment might say ...

(1) The death penalty is barbaric and cruel punishment, hardly the measure of a civilized society.

(2) The death penalty is illogical: In order to show that killing is wrong, we are going to take the people who kill other people and subsequently kill them?

(3) Life imprisonment would send a stronger message against violent crime, because then the criminal would have to live bearing the consequences of his actions for the rest of his life.

(4) The death penalty has been administered to innocent people who have been wrongly accused and put to death.

(5) No matter what, the death penalty will never provide true closure for the victim's family and loved ones. Sadly, nothing will bring the victim back to life.

(6) The Old Testament legitimacy of capital punishment is superseded by Jesus' command of forgiveness in Matthew 5:39 that if someone attacks you and strikes you on your right cheek, the correct thing is to 'turn to him the other one also.'

People who are in favor of proper use of the death penalty might say …

(1) At least in the United States, lethal injection—and the moving away from electrocution and gassing—means that executions are hardly cruel and barbaric.

(2) Is the death penalty illogical? Isn't the issue that it's wrong to take *innocent* human life? Once the murderer commits his act, doesn't he technically forfeit his innocence?

(3) If we imprison murderers and violent criminals for life, justice isn't fully done nor is it exact. Justice should be proportional and swift (while allowing for the legal system to work things out in court), and that provides a more effective message against crime.

(4) Given the advances in DNA testing and forensic science over the years, we can surely eliminate almost all doubt about the guilt of the accused.

(5) The death penalty may not completely heal the wound of grief for those who have lost their loved one. But it can still provide some measure of closure, which is better than none at all.

(6) Jesus' 'turn the other cheek' comment in Matthew 5:39 is not in the context of physical violence and life-threatening attack, but rather is dealing with how the Christian should handle being insulted. Therefore, this passage is not an argument against the death penalty.

'Now What?': Things to Consider

As I said previously, where you land on this issue, as a critic or supporter, is not my primary focus. My concern happens to be the things on which we should agree. Practical responses will not be easy; we are dealing with human beings, and the tendency to sin afflicts the human heart in ways that will always sadden us. Yet if we are committed to bringing *shalom,* God's desires and design, into this world, we need to make constructive attempts.

First, if you accept the authority of the Bible, it is true that there are many statements throughout Scripture that affirm the use of the death penalty. But you must also acknowledge there are a number of places in the Bible where one is *not put to death* for their actions. In Genesis 4 (mentioned previously), God confronts Cain before the murder by warning him to get ahold of his raging emotions and sinful tendencies. And then after the murder, God confronts him again with the facts and that the evil demands a reckoning. But then, notice that God finally confronts Cain with mercy, exiling him instead of killing him while also setting him apart for protection lest anyone take vengeance on Cain. In 2 Samuel 11-12, the same king David who was described as a 'man after God's own heart' orchestrates a murder-for-hire against the military man Uriah so David can snag Uriah's widow Bathsheba for himself. The prophet Nathan angrily confronts David, who exhibits sorrow and remorse, that there will be a life required for the killing. But it is the son born to David and Bathsheba who dies, not David. And in John 8, the Pharisees bring a woman caught in adultery to Jesus, with the reminder that according to their law she should die. After a few hard words directed to the accusers, Jesus is left alone with the woman, to whom He gives the gentle words of hope: 'Neither do I condemn you; go, and from now on, sin no more.'[12] In each case, there is no capital punishment.

---

12. By the way, Jesus' words are a beautiful summary of the hope of a Christian believer. Divine acceptance and reception precede spiritual growth; Jesus doesn't demand that we clean ourselves up first before He receives us. There's a reason He doesn't say, 'Sin no more, and then I won't condemn you.'

Another important suggestion is to ask the question 'What conditions can we address that will curb the tendency toward violence in the communities around us?' It is one thing to have a process of accountability and justice for violent crime. It is another to move beyond this and take care of such problems on the front end. Some individuals and groups call for greater regulation of firearms; others point out that tighter gun control zones result in the higher homicide rates, and criminals will not follow the law anyway. But surely isn't there latitude between these two positions, where it's worth affirming that the use of any potentially lethal weapon carries with it a tremendous sense of responsibility and need for training?

Promoting and supporting strong families is another essential ingredient of building healthy social environments which can push back against the tendency to crime. Almost all reputable studies draw a noticeable link between poverty and unhealthy home life on one hand and crime and incarceration on the other. While there are certainly exceptions to the rule in which people might still flourish,[13] it is true that the best antidote to violent crime in the future tends to include the following ingredients: (a) a two-parent household; (b) children receive both high expectations and unconditional love; (c) parents demonstrate through word and action that wisdom, not abuse or rage, is the key to navigating life's circumstances; and (d) time spent together is valued highly. Not every young person will have this experience. That is why we need to be sensitive to those who are falling through the cracks. Teachers have an opportunity to mentor difficult students and shape their lives in a more enriching direction. Athletic coaches can provide the

---

13. For instance, there are many single parents who are very diligent, loving, and conscientious, and their children grow up to be well-rounded, outstanding members of the community.

discipline, high expectations, and team-building outlets young people need to construct an approach to life that seeks to solve difficulties rather than inflict pain on others.

One other connection that comes to mind has to do with the policing agencies in our communities. It is critical that citizens give honor and respect to those who serve as police and detectives in a given area. But we should also expect that those employed as policemen and policewomen are involved in the communities and proactively build relationships with those who dwell in those places. Law enforcement rightly expects people to uphold what is right, noble, and good, but the desire to do the right thing can thrive best when healthy relationships connect these two parties.

Perhaps you might think this is an overwhelming task. It's true. You won't save the world by your limited actions. You are just one person. But your attempts can still move the 'shalom meter' of God's world in the right direction. It might be in the midst of a one-on-one relationship with an at-risk person; it could be in your attempts to bring justice and hope to larger organizations or to the political realm. Ultimately, promoting the dignity of life is within your reach in the decisions you make every day. As one of our friends is fond of saying, hope begins with one.

For Your Consideration

- Murder is especially horrific. People who are Christian, Jewish, pagan, or non-religious (among others) can be equally repulsed by the tragedy of the unjust taking of human life. What do you think it is that causes such a wide variety of people to be unified about the evil of murder?

- What is your personal view on the death penalty? What are your reasons for your position?

- What do you find to be the strongest reasons for and against the death penalty? The weakest reasons? Why?

- The author asks: 'What conditions can we address that will curb the tendency toward violence in the communities around us?' In your opinion, what are the situations we need to deal with and improve, and how would engagement with these matters build a society that respects life?

6

Abortion

*A*BORTION is a flashpoint topic, capable of sparking a brush fire of words that tend to offer more heat than light. It is a subject that divides people who ordinarily might find much else in common. People of all faiths or none exhibit strong feelings about abortion, but does that automatically mean they've carefully considered all the labels, questions, and realities that come with the territory?

First of all, abortion is not a recent issue, but is rather an action with a history spanning at least forty-five centuries. A royal declaration in China around 2500 B.C. makes mention of it, and the Greek philosopher Aristotle wrote that unwanted embryos should be destroyed rather than brought to full term. The presence of abortion throughout the ancient, medieval, and modern worlds brought a consensus of commentary by Christian leaders against its practice. The ancient preacher St John Chrysostom called abortion worse than murder, 'since it does not take off the thing being born, but prevents its being born.'[1] Thomas Aquinas—though believing the unborn child did not have a soul until it began to move in the womb—also believed abortion was morally

---

1. Chrysostom, *Homily 24 on Romans*.

wrong.[2] The Protestant Reformer John Calvin compared abortion to the killing of a man in his own house, implying the unborn child has every right to feel safe in the womb of her mother.[3] During the American Civil War, twenty states had laws limiting abortion, and feminist Susan B. Anthony spoke out against abortion in her 1875 speech, 'Social Purity.' All of these events occurred well before the United States Supreme Court case of *Roe v. Wade* (and its connected case *Doe v. Bolton*) expanded abortion's legality. So, abortion is hardly a shockingly new topic.

'What?': Defining Abortion

First, some clarity. We can define abortion as *the intentional termination of a human pregnancy*. It is my goal to make the case that we can further qualify abortion as *the willful destruction of an unborn human child*. That sounds harsh to some, but in reality, I propose it is accurate; ideally, we'll unpack that as we go along.

In spite of this hoped-for clarification, there remains much confusion and un-necessary labeling of others. Opponents of abortion call those who differ from them 'pro-aborts' or 'pro-death' while abortion supporters label the other side 'anti-choice' and deniers of liberty. This is what I meant earlier by more heat than light. I think it's helpful to think of these viewpoints as four different tribes.

Pro-abortion: PAs (for lack of a better abbreviation) would hold that abortion should be an unrestricted right for any woman, at any stage of pregnancy, for any reason she chooses. There should be no regulations on abortion at all.

---

2. https://www.nytimes.com/2017/05/11/opinion/aquinas-and-abortion.html

3. Calvin made these statements in his commentary volume on Exodus, in particular looking at 21:22 of that book.

Pro-choice: PCers tend to believe that a woman should have the right to all medical decisions about her body. Abortion should be a personal decision that a woman should make after consultation, and it is a procedure that should be safe, legal, and rare. Note those words. PCers desire abortion to be legal so that it can be done properly by licensed physicians and thus safe for the woman's health. But they tend to want abortion to be rare; many pro-choice people do not like abortion, nor do they want it to be a preferred method of birth control. Yet they want the woman to have the final *choice.*

Pro-life: Properly understood, pro-lifers believe that all life, from formation to funeral, from womb to tomb, is sacred and must be defended and enhanced. Yes, this means they would speak out against abortion. But it also means pro-lifers would speak out *in favor* of medical advances to cure debilitating diseases. It means providing for the physical, mental, and social needs of the profoundly disabled and the elderly. It requires that we thoughtfully consider how to provide the best health care possible to people. It demands that we reach out to those who suffer from anxiety and depression so that they are socially connected. Thus, abortion is one piece of a pro-life ethic, but there are many others.

Anti-abortion: Though people more properly called pro-life get tagged with this label, anti-abortionists tend to focus on the single issue of abortion at the expense of other matters. Often, much is made of 'making abortion illegal' as if a law forbidding a practice would cleanly wipe it out. More extreme representatives of the anti-abortion movement might advocate bombing abortion clinics or killing abortionist physicians, although these are a microscopic minority amongst the group itself.

Please notice that even as I'm clarifying who is who, these are still broadly defined groups that might have disagreements among their own tribes. Pro-choicers might debate whether or not the government should fund abortion providers with taxpayer money. In the pro-life community, some are against abortion for any reason, some would favor it only when the mother's life is clearly at risk during pregnancy or delivery, and some allow for abortion in pregnancies caused by rape or incest.

'So What?': Clarifying a Biblical View of Abortion

It is true that the Bible speaks overwhelmingly of God viewing people as human from the time they are in the uterus. In Psalm 139:13-14, David rejoices that God 'knitted me together in my mother's womb. I praise you, for I am fearfully and wonderfully made.' David also implies human personhood in Psalm 51 when—after self-reflection and repentance over his own sin— he confesses that he was 'brought forth (developed in the womb) in iniquity.' Elizabeth, the mother of John the Baptist, declares in Luke 1:44 that her unborn child threw a celebratory dance upon hearing that Mary was pregnant with the Savior, Jesus.

Additional locations in Scripture more broadly affirm the sanctity of human life, and these take on automatic importance for those who accept the authority of the Bible **and** believe in the humanity of the unborn (as well as of all people). Any passages that speak against murder would thus apply to abortion, such as the 'You shall not murder' commandment in Exodus 20:13 and Deuteronomy 5:17. God's reminder to Noah in the new post-Flood world rings true: 'And for your lifeblood I will demand a reckoning ... for God made man in his own image' (Gen. 9:5-6).

Early Christian documents—even ones that weren't included in Holy Scripture—display an exact match to the Biblical defense of human life. The *Didache*, circulated before A.D. 300 in many ancient churches, offers these words: '**You shall not murder**

a child by abortion nor kill them when born' (Didache 2:2). Notice the words. They assume the elimination of the unborn and born were on the same level of horrific sin.

I don't mean to move too briskly through those verses (we have previously analyzed some of them in our chapter on murder and capital punishment), but they should give evidence that throughout biblical and early church history, God's people spoke with a unified voice: All human life from fertilization to final breath is God-granted and divinely worthy, and an attack on innocent life is an attack on the God who gave it.

'So What?': Clarifying the Key Question

When you walk into a conversation or debate on abortion (whenever that might be), certain words and phrases get tossed around: 'freedom', 'choice', 'right to choose', among others. Even though well-meaning people use words to powerful effect, we have to ask if they get at the heart of the matter. So, fundamentally we have to ask what an abortion is and what the results are. We've already defined abortion previously. The results—though clearly evident—still bear acknowledging: An unborn being was present, and now that being is not. Thus, we are forced to ask the question, *What is the nature of that being who no longer exists?*

If that being is a non-active blob of cells, or an inanimate parasite inside the mother, or a conglomeration that will not ordinarily turn into a child with human DNA, then what's the debate? There would be no need to justify the right to aborting that being. But if the unborn child is human, then there can be *no possible justification that abortion is morally satisfactory.* That is because if the unborn child is human, the child has human rights, amongst which is the right to life.

So, here's what we need to determine: *When is the unborn fetus a human being?* Even if you think this is an open-and-shut case .... surprise! There are several different views on when someone becomes a human being.

One view comes from Peter Singer, and can charitably be called the **post-birth view** (as it is difficult to see how he would consider the unborn to meet these demands). Singer, who is a professor of ethics at Princeton University, says that to qualify for human rights, one (a) must be aware of itself as a living body over a period of time, (b) can desire and plan for things, (c) must want to go on living, and (d) is a decision-making being who can distinguish between suffering and satisfaction.[4]

Another answer to this question comes from those who state that we must identify the child/fetus as human at the moment of **birth**. The argument goes as follows: The fetus is not a human being while in the mother's womb. However, as soon as it exits the womb, the baby (change of environment leads to a change of identity) qualifies as a human person. Some—though not all—of those who take this view might qualify the fetus as a 'collection of tissues', although I don't see how one can say this about a being that goes through a magnificent amount of growth and complex development during a pregnancy.

Yet another group might say that birth is too arbitrary of a point to say the baby is now a human being with human rights. What is at stake, say others, is the issue of **viability.** They ask, 'Can the child survive outside the womb if it were born at this point of development?' The implication is that if it is clear the fetus/baby would survive and have a significant chance of living after a delivery that would be somewhat premature, then it would be morally wrong to terminate the pregnancy from then on. The other implication is that at any point before viability, there would be nothing wrong with an abortion.

---

4. https://www.independentliving.org/docs5/singer.html

Moving even further back in fetal development, some might say the moment of humanity occurs when the **critical organs are present**. Normally, at six weeks of development, the baby has a heartbeat along with early formation of the brain and central nervous system. Granted, the fetus is the size of a sweet pea, but there is a massive amount of genetic and physical activity going on! As with the previous viewpoint, what is implied is that any time after this juncture, abortion should not be performed, while any point before this, abortion would be allowable.

Finally, there is the view that humanity begins at **conception** (although some might say it happens slightly later when the fertilized egg is *implanted* in the mother's uterus). Briefly stated, when the mother's egg is invaded by the father's sperm, this transaction shapes a distinct, unique human being from that point on. This tends to be the default position of many in the pro-life community.

'Now What?': Choosing the Best Option

There are a number of questions that arise as we sift through these views.

For Professor Singer's **post-birth** view, one chilling question is, 'Who makes the decision on someone being self-aware, willful, decision-making, and capable of knowing if he is happy or hurting?' Is it a physician?[5] An intellectual? Singer himself says that newborns—and some beyond this stage—are incapable of these things and so there is nothing wrong with putting them to death after they are born if so desired. Singer has also used this reasoning to justify 'intentionally ending the life of severely disabled infants.' History is full of harsh lessons

---

5. https://whyevolutionistrue.wordpress.com/2017/07/13/should-one-be-allowed-to-euthanize-severely-deformed-or-doomed-newborns/

of what happens once a class of people in a society decide who has the right to live and who does not because unleashed cruelty is not far behind. Nazi Germany's anti-Semitism is just one example among many.

On the **birth** view, one question that comes up is, 'Doesn't the moment of birth seem to be an artificial line of determination?' Think about what the unborn child looks like and how it is functioning seconds before birth. The physical and mental capacities are working pretty much just as they will after birth. Only the environment will change from in the womb to outside of it (and leaving the umbilical cord behind). To insist that birth is the moment that confers humanity on a being creates an arbitrary point of decision.

The **viability** view is well-meaning, and there is proper concern that an unborn child be at a stage far enough along in development that she has a fighting chance to survive a premature birth. But let's not try to convince ourselves that the moment of viability is a fixed point in every pregnancy. Also, a child's chances of survival upon premature birth will depend on a number of factors. What is the quality of prenatal care in the nation in which it is born? What is the quality of medical care at the time of delivery if a birth is premature? What technological advantages or disadvantages will mother and baby have? In the United States, babies born prematurely at twenty-four weeks of development can have *anywhere from a 66 to 80 per cent chance of survival.*[6] The better medical care has gotten, the better chances premature babies have. But in developing nations where medical quality lags, the chances aren't as good. Are we to believe that the possibility of abortion should be extended in those nations to later in pregnancy? Does that make proper sense?

---

6. https://www.verywellfamily.com/what-is-a-micro-preemie-2748625

The opinion that human personhood begins when *critical organs are present* appears to have some merit. After all, it is hard to imagine one surviving well without a heart or a brain. But incidents of fetuses without these organs are microscopically rare. The question then is, does human personhood <u>depend</u> on these organs being in place? Or does it depend on something else?

Let's consider, then, our remaining option: *Life begins at conception.* Scripture overwhelmingly plants the flag firmly in defending the sacredness of all human life from its initial construction. But what if someone says, 'You might believe the Bible is true, but I don't.' What then? Can you (for lack of a better phrase) 'take God out of the equation' and still make a case that an unborn child at any stage is a human person?

I would offer the following to make that case:

(1) If a human mother gives birth to her child, there is no doubt the child is human. And if that child is human at birth, he or she would have to possess potential to become more and more the 'finished product' we see at birth. If someone has the potential to be something, that 'somethingness' would have to be in the core of their being in some measure the entire time. So, a child who is human at birth was truly human all along.

(2) Any being produces offspring of the same nature as that being. A wolf produces wolf cubs, not mountain goats; a salmon produces more salmon, not elephants; a sun bear produces sun bears, not eagles. A human being produces beings with human nature, and that takes us back to the argument in point 1.

(3) Imagine if you would that a space probe on Mars discovers a globule of cellular mush moving along the reddish surface of that planet. The cellular mush seems

to contain division and growth within its 'stuff.' I have no doubt this would be a well-documented achievement, as it should be. Can you imagine the headlines in newspapers, magazines, and online articles? Maybe something like 'Scientists Discover Life Beyond Earth'? Here's my point: If we would call that life, then why wouldn't we grant a growing, highly complex, dividing-yet-expanding group of living cells in a human womb the same designation? It seems hypocritical not to!

'Now What?': Crafting a Practical Response

It's one thing to talk about this topic in theory. But unless you are willing to put your beliefs into practice they will remain theoretical. It is one thing to know *what* is right, it is another to see that it is important and answers the question *'So what?'* But *now what* can we do practically every day?

First of all, the matter of abortion strikes at the very core of what we believe about a human being in general *and about our humanity in particular.* If someone has an abortion, have they eliminated a parasitic lump from their body's interior, as if clipping away a tumor? Or is this a living human child, just obscured by the womb? Also, can someone have a procedure like an abortion under the 'my body, my choice' mantra? Does that not betray a belief that you can keep your body separate from who you are as a person?[7] As I write this, we are just over a month beyond the moment when the New York state legislature legalized abortion all the way up to birth, while a bill of similar magnitude in Virginia failed to come for a vote, but not without lack of effort.[8] Through recent legislative attempts abortion

---

7. For an excellent criticism of this, see Nancy Pearcey's *Love Thy Body.*

8. https://www.vox.com/2019/2/1/18205428/virginia-abortion-bill-kathy-tran-ralph-northam

advocates are betraying that any concern for the 'health of the mother' is hardly on the radar. It doesn't matter how one defines the baby anymore; more abortion advocates are boldly wanting abortion on demand.

All that being said, if you consider yourself pro-life, you need to show care and concern for the unborn, but you also must expand that further to every stage of life. Aside from the other areas mentioned before, there are other actions that reflect pro-life ethics. A number of people go on medical mission trips or have a desire to open up free or low-cost medical clinics in poor, urban areas. Attorneys or counselors who help people who have been physically or sexually abused are exhibiting pro-life activity. Perhaps you are scientifically interested and want to be in research and development for drugs, surgeries, and materials to combat diseases and disabilities. You can demonstrate compassion, give assistance, and offer living space for pregnant mothers in difficult financial situations but want to keep their baby.

Maybe you think those possibilities are well down the road and need to keep things simple right now. There are plenty of opportunities in your backyard. You can volunteer to organize things, fold clothes, or run errands at a pregnancy support center. Join with others at school and spend an afternoon visiting the elderly at a nursing home, playing board games and listening to war stories! Donate items or your time at a shelter for abused women. Or perhaps you know someone who has had an abortion and is racked with confusion, guilt, or regret. Isn't it proper to befriend and pray with her, offering her God's love and grace?

Whether you are thinking on a grand scale or keeping things simple, don't expect to convince thousands of people to believe in the pro-life understanding of things. Yes, there are those who keep track of legal cases on abortion that move through the courts in America, and others may engage in passionate protests on the anniversary of *Roe v. Wade*. But my advice to you is to be patient. Ultimately the way to convince and change others is step by step and one heart at a time. That takes time, but people often must believe something is good and beneficial before they think it is *right*. So, your (and my) requirement is to show the beauty of a life that seeks to uphold all of life as holy and precious. That takes longer than a protest or a court decision, and you probably won't be on television as a result. In the long run, though, it's more beneficial to build bridges with others in such patient ways.

For Your Consideration

- Many people would classify the abortion issue as being between pro-choice and anti-abortion. How does the classification of four different categories help clarify the matter?

- Do you find the biblical data or the scientific data about the human identity and worth of the fetus more convincing? Why do you say that?

- How convinced are you of the three pro-life arguments that 'take God out of the equation'? What are some other non-religious cases you could make for a pro-life position?

- In what areas might you practically get involved in promoting the rights of the unborn, the disabled, the abused, the elderly, etc.?

7
Euthanasia

IT was December of 2005 that my wife and I stood in a room at Northside Hospital in Atlanta, our children nearby. In a bed sat Christi's grandmother, who—due to the fact she practically raised my wife from her earliest years—she always called her 'Mom', though our kids called her Gigi. Over the past month, Gigi's body had been shutting down, and transfusions weren't keeping up with the blood and fluid loss she had been experiencing. As the doctor told us, 'There is nothing more we can do to stop this from happening.' After discussing things amongst ourselves, we started the paperwork necessary to transfer Gigi to a hospice facility. My wife would stay behind in Atlanta to see her through the upcoming days while I took Joshua and Lindsay back to our home in North Carolina. On the way back, over the remnants of the value menu at Wendy's in Suwanee, Lindsay asked, 'How long before Gigi is able to go home?'

Only the truth calmly told would serve our four-year-old girl. 'Lindsay, sweetie,' I said, 'Gigi will probably die in a few days and we want her to be as happy as possible before she sees Jesus.'

'What?': The End of Life Is Coming

I share that remembrance, not to depress you at the start of a new chapter, but so you might realize there is experience behind what I say here. Each of us has a heart that will stop beating one day. We have family members who are approaching that day sooner than we are, and that means you and I will bear the weight of responsibility for some critical medical decisions. We'll face questions about chances of medical success, about life support, and other queries.

One category for all these questions comes under the term *euthanasia* (yoo-thu-NAY-zjah). Euthanasia comes from the Greek words for 'good death.' When an individual is facing a debilitating illness or disease, and the condition will only worsen, and there is no hope of shifting the balance so that the patient will recover, euthanasia—the allowance of death in an active or passive fashion to stop a person's pain or suffering— is the option that many consider. One challenge, though, that arises for many is that the word *euthanasia* requires more unpacking and forces us to ask some questions.

Some might ask, 'Wait a second. Don't doctors take an oath not to end people's lives?' It is true that physicians take the Hippocratic Oath, although the affirmation to always prescribe regimens for the good of one's patients and to never do harm to anyone were only in the *original oath* penned by Hippocrates. In truth, although medical schools have their graduates swear some sort of professional oath, practically none truly use the actual Hippocratic Oath, instead using a revised oath drawn up by the school.[1]

A second matter has to do with what the subject of euthanasia reveals. Many of the decisions about ending one's life in dire straits are made by the patient. You may happen to oppose some forms of euthanasia (as I do), but the fact that people have these decisions to make shows the level of freedom

---

1. https://www.statnews.com/2016/09/21/hippocratic-oath-medical-students-doctors/

we have to make important choices like these. These may be *difficult* selections, but at least they are, to a great degree, *our* selections.

One final note: Before we discuss an issue (as with others we've encountered), we should define what is meant and what the particular 'tribes' believe. So here we go, as the wider matter of euthanasia encompasses three differing perspectives.

'So What?': Passive Euthanasia Defined

The first subcategory can be labeled *passive euthanasia*. You may remember that part of my initial definition of euthanasia stated it could be done in an active or passive fashion. A passive approach to things means more of a 'hands-off mentality.' Here, neither the patient, the patient's family or loved ones, nor the patient's physician(s) undertake a particular action causing the terminally ill patient to die. Instead, having exhausted all possible means of staving off imminent death, the decision is made to 'allow nature to take its course.'

This can occur in several ways. A man with a traumatic brain injury might have taken such a blow to his central nervous system that there is no true brain wave activity – the brain stem and anything that would help 'run' the rest of the body (keep in mind the brain is one's central computer and requires oxygen to function) are non-operational except for the fact that life support machinery is keeping the man alive. His family may desire to keep him on life support in the hope his brain and spinal cord might re-ignite. There have been a number of cases where people have inexplicably recovered. Physicians can also misdiagnose brain death; they are human, after all. But under normal conditions of what here is called 'brain death', the chance of recovery is minimal, and even then, might result in a permanent vegetative state. It is in these cases that removing life support is an agreeable choice.

This can also be the case with those in truly irreversible conditions in which death is imminent if no continued heroic measures are taken. As mentioned at the start of this chapter, our family has lived through this in the situation with Gigi. The blood transfusions were not dialing back the suffering but only prolonging the inevitable. And my statement to Lindsay that Sunday afternoon was correct. Gigi died four days later. We did not cause her death with our decision to move her into hospice. I don't believe you can even say we *hastened* her death. That would have involved a proactive step to give her something to bring it on. Instead, we—recognizing we could do nothing to stop the onslaught her body was executing against herself— allowed what was truly inevitable to happen, and Gigi was placed in hospice care with a carefully prescribed morphine drip to keep her comfortable over her last days.

We must exercise caution here. What one might label 'passive' can really be masking a desire to just give up and is no different than outright neglect. Our son Joshua bears the neuro-muscular disorder known as X-linked myotubular myopathy. A scant percentage of boys afflicted with this disease live past the age of ten. During the summer of 2007, when Josh was a half-year shy of ten years of age, his disorder had caused his spine to curve so badly he required surgery. His recovery was so long and so difficult that there were a couple times we wondered if he'd survive (including a harrowing weekend when he was practically hours from death). After some time, at least one doctor in the pediatric critical care unit moved from wonder to outright doubt. One morning during rounds, he spoke to my wife. Granted he addressed her, not Joshua, but our son didn't need to perk up his usual excellent hearing to notice this (Joshua can probably hear a cotton ball being laid on a bed of macaroni). The doctor point-blank told my wife, 'You know, you may have to face that the time has come to take him home and let nature take its course.'

For the record, my wife did not accept that at all. At all. Joshua's recovery was slow, but he was not terminal. And he certainly wasn't getting worse. The doctor had truly overstepped the bounds in suggesting that to Christi. He was merely trying to make room for another patient he deemed worthier of saving. To him, Joshua was a roadblock.

Hopefully, you see the clear distinction between these two scenarios. With my mother-in-law, she was terminal; Joshua was not. The key question in each case was, 'Can we save _____'s life?' And that's the difference in what makes passive euthanasia allowable or not.[2] And there seems to be nothing wrong with the use of drugs and properly managed painkillers to help the terminally ill suffer less as they approach death's door. In Proverbs 31:6, King Lemuel writes that it can be wise to '[g]ive strong drink to the one who is perishing, and wine to those in bitter distress.' In short, a product to stiff-arm abject pain is entirely understandable. A comfortable road to one's final breath is completely agreeable.

'So What?': Assisted Suicide Defined

The waters get significantly muddied when we speak of assisted suicide. Here I am lumping together two separate actions into one for the purpose of discussion. Either a physician will prescribe a drug for the terminally ill patient to take for the purpose of causing death (usually a 9000 mg dosage of secobarbital in capsule form[3]) or the physician might administer

---

2. Notice I said 'allowable', not 'commanded'. No one *needs* to remove someone from life support or deny heroic measures, although patients who have a 'do not resuscitate' measure in legal force cannot be kept alive through such measures. One can seek to hope for the best and keep a loved one alive. But, as said before, in a brain-dead/vegetative state, the chances of revival are so low that we are speaking of a practically irreversible condition. And the cost of keeping someone alive perpetually on life support can be quite cost-prohibitive.

3. http://www.patientsrightscouncil.org/site/2017-summary-of-drugs-used-for-doctor-prescribed-suicide/

the drug himself in states where this is legalized.[4] Death-with-dignity advocates argue for the legitimacy of assisted suicide as a way of providing positive experiences for people who will die, especially in a great deal of pain. A number of (not all) Christian groups and denominations speak out against assisted suicide, including the Roman Catholic Church and many Protestant evangelical denominations.

There are several arguments advanced in favor of assisted suicide. Among those are the following:

(1) It is morally wrong to force the terminally ill to die slowly and painfully. This cheapens their personal dignity and worth.

(2) People have a right to full freedom and autonomy to die with dignity. It is their choice to leave life on their own terms.

(3) The family and friends of terminally ill and suffering-wracked individuals can be spared a great deal of agony by watching their dear one experiencing the extended pain and suffering.

(4) Medical care should be truly compassionate. While we would desire to extend this to all people in all cases, in a world of tough choices, true compassion focuses on the patients who can be saved and healed, not the situations that are irreversible.

It's important to note the key words used in the above statements, words like *morally, personal dignity, freedom, spared,* and *compassionate.* Assisted suicide advocates do not approach these matters from a desire to reduce the human population, nor do the overwhelming majority of them believe there are people who

---

4. Eight states, if you count Montana's court ruling. See https://www.deathwithdignity.org/learn/death-with-dignity-acts/

are sub-human and unworthy of life (the previously-mentioned Peter Singer notwithstanding). Their wishes embrace a vision for human life that they believe is good. And the decision for assisted suicide can arise within some devastating moments. Behind every argument on an issue is a human dilemma.

A few years back, Brittany Maynard was a vibrant young lady with a college degree in hand (psychology major) and a passion to travel and serve internationally. The California native taught at an orphanage in Nepal and traveled throughout southeast Asia.[5] In September 2012, at twenty-seven years of age, Brittany married her husband Daniel, with the bright hope they would begin a family soon. Those desires came crashing down in January 2014, when she sat in a doctor's office in California, receiving the news about why she'd been experiencing such crushing headaches. The reason: She had grade 2 astrocytoma, a form of brain cancer which required a craniotomy to rest her brain's temporal lobe. Even with radiation treatments, the cancer returned to grade 4 status in April of that year, and her doctor told her she had six months to live. Medication designed to shrink the tumor and provide some relief only caused her body tissues to expand, with no respite from the debilitating pain. Brittany thought about living out her remaining days in a hospice, but then she spurned that in favor of other choices. She and Daniel moved to Oregon, where assisted suicide was legal. She traveled around America during her final months with her husband at her side. Together they visited Yellowstone National Park, the wilds of Alaska, and finally the breathtaking beauty of the Grand Canyon.[6] The memories were exquisite and sweeping

---

5. https://people.com/celebrity/brittany-maynard-death-with-dignity-ended-her-own-life/

6. https://www.news.com.au/lifestyle/real-life/brittany-maynard-ticks-off-some-items-on-her-bucket-list-before-she-dies-with-dignity/news-story/

but took a toll on poor Brittany's reserves. In November 2014, with her loved ones present, Brittany took her prescribed fatal medication to pass from her earthly life.

I don't share that story to shame you into making the most of your life, or to speak out in favor of assisted suicide (I am, in fact, against it), but to make you aware that many folks reach these decisions through a great deal of anguish, and even if you *oppose* their conclusions, you can at least *empathize* with their situations.

Yet empathy is not the sum of truth.

'Now What'?: A Vision for Finishing Well

The four assisted suicide arguments I gave previously do not stand unopposed. People who do not advocate assisted suicide (and who might strongly advocate for passive euthanasia) might offer the following:

(1) Suffering can be redemptive. This is not to say you should aim for some cathartic masochism or seek out medical hardship. But there can be many teachable moments we discover through pain.

(2) Doctors can be very insightful, but doctors can also be wrong at times, even when assuming a patient may never recover. As I shared above regarding the doctor who was dismissive of our son's recovery, they can be very far afield of reality.

(3) Do we truly have full freedom and autonomy? If we did, the extent of our ability and wisdom would be super-extensive. Obviously, we are not truly fully free and autonomous.[7]

---

7. Even God is not free to do absolutely everything. He can't do self-contradictory things because only foolish beings would do so. He can't sin because only weak, stupid beings commit sin or mistakes. Because God is all-powerful, all-knowing, and all-loving, there are some things that by virtue of

We discover our freedom when we live according to the design of our Creator rather than prodding against the way in which He has constructed us.[8]

(4) Can't we say the sanctity of human life is an absolute truth with no exception here? If we say that we can determine a point when life is not worth living, we are technically playing the role of God, which is not ours to play.

(5) And even though I'm wary of slippery slope arguments (e.g., if you do X, eventually it will result in Y), we have to beware that voluntary death-with-dignity has morphed into an involuntary mode elsewhere. This has been the case in the Netherlands for some time with the Groningen Protocol, which allows for a doctor to end the life of an infant under the age of one year old.[9] One can't help but wonder if the door is opened to this point, how does one justify stopping its momentum?

All this is to say there are several reasons to demonstrate that the weight of Biblical truth and the sacredness of human life press against the legitimacy of assisted suicide, while preserving the allowance of passive euthanasia given proper

---

who God is, He can't do! It is better to say that God is completely free to do all things *that are consistent within His divine nature.*

8. John Stott wisely raised these matters in his *Issues Facing Christians Today, 4th edition* (Grand Rapids, MI: Zondervan, 2006), p. 414.

9. According to the law, termination of the infant's life is allowable if (a) hopeless and unbearable suffering is verified, (b) the parents consent to the termination, (c) medical consultation takes place, (d) the termination is carefully accomplished, and (e) the doctor who ends the life of the baby reports it to the medical examiner. See Verhagen, AA.; Sol, JJ.; Brouwer, OF.; Sauer, PJ. (Jan. 2005). '[Deliberate termination of life in newborns in The Netherlands; review of all 22 reported cases between 1997 and 2004]'. Ned Tijdschr Geneeskd. 149 (4): 183–8.

parameters. I should also say that such end-of-life issues afford an opportunity for followers of Jesus to inhabit this process. Perhaps you are a student who leans more toward the sciences; you might consider going into pharmaceutical development, contributing to treatments for terminal illnesses or drugs for pain management. Maybe you have a heart for those who are facing down an irreversible condition or disease and can provide hope and companionship for however long or short they might have left on earth. Medical or hospice chaplaincy might be something you consider for your future. People who have lost their loved ones also require soul care, and it could be that you might consider bereavement counseling as a vocational field.

Regardless of where you might be headed in the future, chances are you might intersect with some of these hard decisions at some point. And it would be helpful to recall that in all things, we are dependent upon our Creator and our lives should be offerings of gratitude to Him, even if we bear an irreversible illness within our bodies. I write these words on the two-year anniversary of the death of Hella Smith, the wife of my friend and colleague Warren Smith. Hella was diagnosed with a brain tumor, dealt with it surgically, and after initially promising news it—like Brittany Maynard's in a different sense—returned to retreat no more. Yes, Warren and Hella took some travels together to Wisconsin, South Dakota, and Montana, until Hella's tumor proved too debilitating. For eight weeks, Warren took time away from teaching biology at our school to care for his dear wife, who never complained, who loved it when people from church visited, and who always was grateful for being Jesus' child. Hella died on May 11, 2017, as she had lived, with joy and purpose, at last passing into the arms of her Savior Jesus. That is death with dignity, at the close of a God-enriched life of great dignity.

For Your Consideration

- In your opinion, what might make end-of-life decisions—whether for you or your loved ones—so difficult?

- What connections do you see between someone's view of the value of life and their view on end-of-life decisions? How do you explain that?

- Look at the arguments for and against assisted suicide. Which do you believe are the strongest/weakest for each side? Why do you say that?

- The author says that 'even if you *oppose* their conclusions, you can at least *empathize* with their situations.' Why is empathy so important and powerful for those going through these moments? How might you express kind understanding even if you firmly disagree with someone else's position on euthanasia?

8

Despair and Suicide

IT was a hot Missouri day in July 2017, and I was driving through the streets of St Charles with my daughter Lindsay in the passenger seat. My mobile phone jangled and, in spite of the fact I was driving, I answered it. It was my wife, after all, who was calling.

But I wasn't prepared for the sound emanating from the other end of the line. Christi was crying bitterly, barely able to get her words out. Asking her to repeat herself and straining to hear the choked verbiage, I caught her saying, 'Chester Bennington killed himself!'

Celebrity deaths may or may not smash into everyone like a boulder, but this hit us with the full force of a hurricane. Chester Bennington was the lead singer for the band Linkin Park. We had played a beautiful Linkin Park tune at our son's funeral nine years before, and we loved their music. So, the news of Chester's tragic decision pounded us extremely hard. A married man with three children, Chester could not shake the depression and despair that was the residue of a childhood marked by sexual abuse. Unable to find a way out from his torment and pain, Chester chose to take his own life so that the anguish might end for good.

And this is neither an isolated event nor a matter reserved only for human headliners. Terrible sadness floods the souls of people we know (and even ourselves, for those who battle these issues). If you don't know someone who has committed or attempted suicide, you at least know someone who knows another who has. So many of us are on the front lines when it comes to these matters.

Yet being on the front lines does not mean we go into the battle without any direction from God. We have already dealt with the issue of murder, an act which is clearly condemned by God. Suicide is connected to this principle: As all life is sacred and precious, we have no right to take innocent human life, and that includes our own lives. Suicide is *never* God's intended solution for life's pain, and we should do everything in our power to prevent others (including ourselves if we are slipping deeply into such despair) from taking that fatal step.

'What?': The Reality of Suicide

The taking of one's life does not occur in a vacuum. The overwhelming majority of suicide cases are the result of long-standing major depression, bipolar disorder, severe anxiety, or other mental and psychiatric matters. These are not challenges to fight alone, and isolation will only underscore and heighten the difficult battles already underway.[1] Depression and anxiety are on the rise amongst younger generations for a variety of reasons,[2] so knowing how to help others navigate this terrain is especially critical. These are conditions that can be attributed to past trauma in the life of a person, or—for reasons beyond figuring out—someone might just have a frazzled

---

1. While we'll mention a number of strategies for combating depression and suicidal thoughts in the 'Now What?' section, it's not wise to employ the strategy of just toughing it out and getting through it on your own.

2. https://www.healthline.com/health-news/millennial-depression-on-the-rise#Millennial-who?

level of neurotransmitters like serotonin[3] or dopamine in the bloodstream, thus affecting one's mood.

Suicide has garnered a checkered analysis throughout human history. The Bible mentions cases of it through the bitter deaths of people such as King Saul and his armor-bearer (1 Sam. 31:4-5), Ahithophel (2 Sam. 17:23), and Judas (Matt. 27:1-10). However, Judas is the only one where we get a window into his mental state before he takes his life, as his remorse over betraying Jesus played the significant role. While Jewish rabbis of the Talmud era disallowed any funeral rites for victims of suicide,[4] more recent Jewish scholarship has demonstrated increasing compassion, especially for those who must live on after the tragic death of their loved one. Ancient Greece tended to dissuade suicide, for the reason that it deprived democracy of useful citizens, and in some cultures through the Middle Ages it was labeled as a crime, where those who took their own life were denied a Christian burial.[5]

We can't overturn the views of the past, but we can face some tough realities in the present. Globally, nearly 800,000 people on the planet die by suicide in each calendar year. As staggering as that number is, it's equally heart-rending to note that that works out to nearly one suicide every forty *seconds*. According to the best data culled by the Centers for Disease Control, there are *twenty-four unsuccessful* suicide attempts in the United States for every committed suicide, which indicates there is significant emotional pain and despair present in the lives of people.[6] Suicide is the tenth leading cause of death in

3. https://www.medicalnewstoday.com/kc/serotonin-facts-232248

4. https://www.jewishvirtuallibrary.org/suicide

5. https://web.archive.org/web/20070317103747/http://pipsproject.com/Understanding%20Suicide.html

6. www.save.org/about-suicide/suicide-facts

the United States,[7] and amongst young people ages 15-24, it remains a highly tragic statistic:

- In the U.S., suicide is the third leading cause of death for young people ages 15-24.[8]

- In Canada, it is the second leading cause of death for the same age category.[9]

- In Australia, it ranked first in recent years in the cause of death for teenagers and young adults.[10]

In addition, the Suicide Awareness Voices in Education notes that—at least in the United States—females are twice as likely to experience depression and have suicidal thoughts and three times more likely to *attempt* suicide than males. Yet males *commit* suicide at a rate three to four times higher than females (this trend of male suicide outranking female action is the tendency worldwide, with China being a notable exception). Gay and lesbian teens and transgendered adults are more highly prone to suicidal thoughts and attempts than the average population.[11]

There are some echoes of hope in various locales. In the United Kingdom, the male suicide rate has significantly decreased in

---

7. https://afsp.org/about-suicide/suicide-statistics/

8. www.save.org/about-suicide/suicide-facts

9. http://teenmentalhealth.org/learn/suicide/

10. https://healthyfamilies.beyondblue.org.au/age-13/mental-health-conditions-in-young-people/suicide

11. In addition to SAVE, there are many websites where you can cull the data on various national statistics on suicide. The World Health Organization has a user-friendly tool for those who want to research this area. Keep in mind, though, that not every nation will have turned over their most recent data. Also note that we are stressing the suicide *rate*, which is all suicides taken out of every 100,000 people. Therefore, a place like Greenland will have amongst the highest rates despite having a very small population, whereas China will have a high raw number of suicides merely due to their population rank.

recent years to the lowest rate since the late 1980s, and in the Republic of Ireland, the suicide numbers and rate have fallen for both genders.[12] Suicide prevention organizations such as Samaritans in the U.K. do yeoman work in giving struggling people hope. Suicide prevention hotlines in the United States exist to grant those in despair a listening ear just a phone call away.

All of this is not meant to be a mere tidal wave of data. We need to take from these facts a sober understanding that there is much pain present in the lives of others and ourselves who struggle with these matters.

'So What?': The Causes of Suicide

It's only fair to mention that for every individual who has encountered suicidal thoughts or desires, there is a different story for each person. There are some common threads that serve as risk factors, though. But we do a disservice to those who suffer and who consider suicide by reducing matters to the idea that 'they just want to kill themselves.' This is neither fair nor accurate. People who seriously entertain thoughts of suicide are overwhelmed by hardship and despair and believe that any chance of rescue from their trauma is hopeless.[13] Eventually, one can inhabit a sense of 'tunnel vision', where the heavy load of despair becomes weightier and one's prospects for release become darker. In truth, the suicidal person *does not primarily think in terms of killing oneself. He or she is desperate for the pain to end, and suicide seems like the only path to wholeness.*

---

12. https://www.samaritans.org/about-samaritans/research-policy/suicide-facts-and-figures/

13. Many of the details in this section come from the Mayo Clinic at https://www.mayoclinic.org/diseases-conditions/suicide/symptoms-causes/syc-20378048

As stated before, medical conditions or psychiatric disorders can play a significant role in a possible path toward suicidal ideation. This is not to say that everyone who battles depression, bipolar disorder, massive anxiety, or post-traumatic stress disorder will automatically be suicidal, but these are factors in the majority of suicide cases. These conditions can bring on feelings of hopelessness, helplessness, and worthlessness; left unchecked, these emotions can expand as the person becomes agitated or more isolated from human connections. Irritability combined with loneliness can only cause more beliefs like 'I'm the only one facing this problem' or 'No way anyone would want to help me ... I'd only bring them down.'

Difficult life events like the death of a friend or loved one, the loss of employment, or other experiences can bring on prolonged depression or stress that can lead to thoughts of hopelessness. The bodily chemical interactions resulting from alcohol and drug abuse can make thoughts of suicide even more numerous and the recklessness of substance addiction can morph into the impulsiveness to act out on one's suicidal thoughts. Perhaps one of the most chilling instances that serves as a suicide risk factor is the horror of childhood trauma, especially physical and sexual abuse visited upon young people by adult perpetrators. With little ability or context to process this evil madness, children can grow up harboring depression and anxiety that can increase into the adult years.

Within the last quarter-century, there has been a noticeable link between bullying and suicide. Victims of bullying may have difficulty processing the cruelty done to them, especially if they are school-age children. They might find it extraordinarily difficult to call out such behavior or tell an adult about it; such 'whistleblowing' can result—so they might reason—in more cruelty. Gay and lesbian youth can be particularly as risk sometimes,[14] and every month brings more tragic evidence that students can use social media as an avenue to bully others, even suggesting to their peers to kill themselves.[15]

These issues don't seem to be slowing down, either. Younger generations are exhibiting clinical depression and anxiety at greater rates than previous eras, in both the United Kingdom[16] and the United States.[17] All of this means that we must have a multi-layered, practical strategy to help anyone caught in the throes of helplessness, compassionately leading them from darkness into light.

'Now What?': Bringing Hope

Perhaps now you're asking, 'What can I do to help a suicidal friend?' or 'What would I want someone to say to me?' I can't give you a fully stocked toolkit in just over a couple pages of text, but some of these ideas might serve you well.

The first, and arguably the most critical, resolution I would urge is that we need to be better connected to one another. To be known by others, and to be accepted with all our shortcomings and successes, can reinforce that there are people who will

---

14. Yes, it is the author's contention that homosexual activity is horrendously sinful, but just as certainly, there is no way one can legitimately maintain that bullying LGBTQ individuals is God-honoring. Rather, people should have at least a modicum of compassion for gays, lesbians, and transgendered folk. When we see others resisting the way God has designed us to function, that should provoke sadness more than anger.

15. See https://www.telegraph.co.uk/science/2018/04/22/cyberbullying-makes-young-people-twice-likely-self-harm-attempt/ for a digest of a university study on this topic.

16. https://academic.oup.com/ije/advance-article-abstract/doi/10.1093/ije/dyz006/5366210?redirectedFrom=fulltext

17. Blue Cross/Blue Shield's study showed that depression has recently spiked amongst millennials. See https://www.bcbs.com/sites/default/files/file-attachments/health-of-america-report/HoA_Major_Depression_Report.pdf

fight alongside us in our most vexing battles. One of the most critical mistakes we can make is isolate ourselves from others. Have you noticed peers sliding away from others, being less involved in activities they normally valued, or retreating into themselves (or spending all their time on their iPhones or social media)? Such behavior can be a silent cry for help. People who are clinically depressed or dealing with extended sadness and hopelessness might believe they are isolated and have no allies to help them in their challenges. Invading their space and demonstrating a willingness to navigate life with them shows them they are not alone.

Also, gutting things out on one's own (as I endnote below) is not a wise long-term strategy to battle depression and despair. The best path is to utilize a connection with a licensed professional—either a counselor, psychiatrist, or other kind of psychological therapist—for wisdom, combined with medication that may be required. The medication side of things can be tricky and one might find this is a trial-and-error game. Many prescription drugs are helpful, but not everything is the right fit, depending on what brain chemicals might be giving one trouble. Medications like Paxil, Prozac, Zoloft, Cymbalta, Effexor, Wellbutrin, and others are among the options, but it might take some time to discover the one that 'clicks' the best.[18] As with any prescription drugs, we must be aware of side effects, especially when we have other medications to take. This can be quite important if one is also taking something to combat anxiety, as well. Make sure you do enough research to check for potential conflicts.

Maybe you hear a friend or acquaintance talking or muttering something about killing himself or herself. It might be tempting to pass that off as a joke, an unserious comment, or a

---

18. https://www.healthline.com/health/depression/medication-list

cry for attention. It could be that, yet I think the right decision is to err on the side of caution. Always take these statements seriously, either by talking to the person who said it or involving a trusted person who can speak into the situation wisely. One common thread in many suicides is that the victim had shared their intentions—even cryptically—with someone else they knew. If someone does share these feelings with you, show them their intentions matter to you and that you don't want them to make this fatal choice. Your goal is to offer your friend alternatives, to demonstrate how much you value them and what their friendship means to you. In the process of deflecting him from his intentions, your friend might discover there are people who truly love them well, and that can make all the difference.

In fact, there are many practical methods of engagement here. A number of countries and areas might have emergency telephone numbers, connecting people in emotional distress and on the verge of suicide with trained counselors.[19] There is another program in the United Kingdom designed to engage potentially suicidal folks during the ordinary moments of every day. The Samaritans organization trains thousands of workers in the British railway system to be able to open up conversations with anyone who appears suicidal or despondent; they are empowered to approach anyone at risk and start a conversation. Railway employees have utilized small talk and everyday questions when they notice travelers who look isolated or troubled, and a number of these occurrences have led to extended conversations, admissions of despair and great need, and thus have resulted in saved lives.[20]

---

19. In the United States, for example, the National Suicide Prevention Lifeline is 1-800-273-8255.

20. https://www.samaritans.org/support-us/campaign/small-talk-saves-lives/how-approach-someone-train-platform/

I do want to share one final word about this subject. Sometimes people ask me, *'What about the Christian believer who experiences depression, suicidal thoughts, or who does happen to end their own life? What are we to say to that?'* I know there are a variety of responses to this; I'm going to give you my best guess.

First, Christian believers are not immune from despair or trauma-induced hopelessness. A good portion of the biblical book of Job displays Job's horror and anguish over the loss of all his children, his wealth, and his health, and he wonders aloud how this could happen, even as he desperately tries to hang on to his faith.[21] My wife Christi is a long-time follower of Jesus who nonetheless deals with depression and anxiety for many reasons. I have friends and colleagues who follow Jesus who still manage through a number of valleys of despair and require constant help and encouragement.

Secondly, despair, depression, and pain are not necessarily evidence of God's displeasure of His people nor evidence that they have fallen away from Christ. It is unscriptural to blurt out, 'Well, if you're going through depression, you're obviously not trusting God.' Never—I repeat, never—utter anything that uncharitable and off-target to anyone, especially to a follower of Jesus who is doing all she can to keep trudging on.

I've known of Christians who have committed suicide (including several ministers). Obviously, I hold on to what I said before, that suicide is an action expressly against God's will. Yes, it is a sinful action, but I don't believe it separates one from the Savior. If Jesus' death has indeed paid the penalty for your sin, and if you trust in Christ to rescue you from your rebellion to God, then that identity in Christ is *objective*; it is

---

21. I could go on and on about the value of hardship and pain for believers. For more detailed treatments of these issues, see C. S. Lewis' *The Problem of Pain,* and Philip Yancey's *Where is God When It Hurts?* and *Disappointment With God.*

authentic and consistent because what God has done for you in Jesus has lasting, unbreakable implications. Whatever feelings of depression or despair you may have are *subjective*; they can be true at times, but other times they may not be. Feelings of hopelessness are what we might <u>perceive</u> to be true due to our circumstances. The big truth here is that even when you feel hopeless, because of who Christ is and what He has done for you, hope <u>does exist</u>, even if you don't feel it. It's much like the sun; you would never say it doesn't exist just because it is obscured by dark clouds. No amount of perceived hopelessness nor a tragic action like suicide can take away the fact that you have been rescued by Jesus' death and resurrection. The Cross, not despair nor self-infliction, has the final word. Yes, life can be just as—if not more so—difficult and screwed up *after* you become a follower of Jesus, but you don't have to pretend everything is all sunshine and roses. You can take off the mask. What matters is that you have an Advocate and Companion who truly knows your pain, who took on more pain than we can imagine in His sacrifice.

> *The other gods were strong; but Thou wast weak;*
> *They rode, but Thou didst stumble to a throne;*
> *But to our wounds only God's wounds can speak,*
> *And not a god has wounds, but Thou alone.*[22]

For Your Consideration

- Conditions of loneliness and depression that lead to despair and suicide are on the rise. What do you think accounts for this?

- The author states, 'In truth, the suicidal person *does not primarily think in terms of killing oneself. He or she is*

---

22. From 'Jesus of the Scars' by Edward Shillito.

<u>*desperate for the pain to end*</u>, *and suicide seems like the only path to wholeness.'* How does this influence how you might help a friend who is battling suicidal thoughts?

- As you think about helping people who have lost hope, what is the greatest challenge you think you'd face in that process? Why do you say that? How can you become a dependable person for others in despair or depression?

9
Disabilities and Dignity

I still remember the phone call in December of 1997. Two days before, my wife had given birth to our first child, our son Joshua. While our heads were still spinning joyfully over our newly minted parenthood, it was clear that Joshua's birth was, well, hardly normal. When he went to take his initial cry after his womb exit, his mouth opened but no sound came out. His arms and legs, instead of bunching tensely near his torso and abdomen, hung loosely like sausage links in a butcher shop window. A couple of specialists opined that tests needed to happen, and then I—having returned to school for a day during exam week—happened to call after Christi had received some fairly stunning news. Fresh tears choked her voice as she explained that all indications were that Joshua had some sort of muscular disorder; hence, his failure to hold his head up, his floppy appearance, and so on. I'll never forgot how Christi wailed out the words, '*It's a genetic defect, honey, and he was born with it!*'

Our plunge into the world of physical disability was far from over. As time went on, we discovered that Joshua had a rare disorder called myotubular myopathy,[1] which he received

---

1. For more information, check out www.joshuafrase.org

thanks to an X-linked gene (from Mom) tweak during fetal development. Thanks to a lack of a certain protein, Joshua had pronounced muscular weakness. After three more years, we had a beautiful daughter Lindsay, followed by another myopathy-affected son seven years after Lindsay's birth, named Jordan. We were a family marked by physical disability, as Joshua and Jordan had the disorder and Christi carried the gene (and who knows if Lindsay carries it, too). Even then, the hardship was far from over. On November 23, 2008, after a bout with pneumonia, little Jordan died suddenly and peacefully at our home, his nineteen-month fight on earth having run its course.

'What?': The reality of pain

Our story of disability is one out of a billion, almost literally. The World Health Organization estimated that about 15 per cent of the planet's human population lives with some form of physical disability, and upwards of a quarter of that subset function at a significantly impaired level.[2] Given that physical disabilities and genetic disorders advance across geographical and economic barriers, it should not surprise us that a large number of the world's disabled live without access to the care, management, and medical services they require.

Adding to this, we have several other factors. There are people who suffer from disabilities, such as learning differences, verbal and communicative disorders, and other matters, that aren't physical in the same sense of a mobility impairment, blindness, or deafness, but which present challenges to how one navigates through life. Other complications occur in the bizarre activities of some who intentionally harm themselves and claim disability

2. https://www.who.int/disabilities/world_report/2011/report/en/

(rare, but known to happen),[3] and the more prevalent issue of the bullying of people with disabilities.[4]

In spite of these challenges, perhaps the most significant change in the past fifty years is the shifting perception of society's view of people with disabilities, as well as greater self-advocacy by those who are disabled. For the great majority of human history, many have positioned the blind, lame, deaf, mute, and otherwise afflicted on the margins of society far from the center. How is it, many might imply by their actions, that such people could muster meaningful contributions to the community at large? Don't the severe physical impairments prevent such folks from benefiting the world around them in a noticeable way? Are these individuals more liability than potential legacy? All these questions tend to be unspoken ones, but throughout the history of the world, actions have spoken louder than words. The good news is that people generally verbalize 'disability rights' and highlight the meaningful work of the disabled more now than ever before. Any discrimination against disabled people was prohibited by law in the United States via passage of the Americans With Disabilities Act in 1990. The heart of this legislation guaranteed 'equal opportunity for individuals with disabilities in public accommodations, employment, transportation, state and local government services, and telecommunications.'[5] People with disabilities have risen to the forefront of their fields in the workforce. Examples include

3. https://www.usatoday.com/story/life/people/2018/11/01/better-call-saul-actor-cut-off-arm-pretended-wounded-vet-todd-lawson-latourette/1844593002/

4. Such as the actions of schoolchildren. Witness https://www.washington post.com/nation/2018/11/13/laughing-teens-make-boy-with-cerebral-palsy-lie-muddy-creek-using-him-human-bridge-he-forgives-them/?noredirect=on&utm_term=.aa536c089fb0

5. https://adata.org/learn-about-ada

the late astrophysicist Stephen Hawking (wheelchair bound with ALS), actor Michael J. Fox (Parkinson's disease), musician and tenor Andrea Boccelli (blind), and Christian motivational speaker Nick Vujicic (no arms or legs).

Nevertheless, people with disabilities can endure a significant amount of pain, loneliness, and hardship. Such individuals can be the most at risk when it comes to high medical costs. Homebound, less mobile people can experience deep loneliness due to lack of contact with others. Also, the unemployment rate for the disabled is nearly 66 per cent (thankfully, that number has been decreasing).[6] In spite of many strides on behalf of the disabled, much ground remains to provide even greater opportunities.

'So What?': The Precious Nature of the disabled

Knowledge of the plight of others is essential, of course, but there is also the need to be moved to action. Why, one might ask, should our compassion be directed to those who are compromised in such ways?

The Christian tradition raises a great deal of hope for those whose experience is that of physical shortcomings. Jesus Christ Himself set the standard for how one should extend compassion and hope. The Gospel writers of the New Testament spill a great deal of ink showing how Jesus desired the company of 'the least of these' over any chance to rub elbows with the leaders and celebrities of His day.

Notice Matthew 14. Jesus is enjoying a stretch of alone time in an offshore boat when a large swath of people invade His space. Practically speaking, they barge in on Him, having traveled quite some distance from the surrounding towns and now they're arrayed along the shore within earshot. Evidently,

---

6. https://www.bls.gov/news.release/disabl.nr0.htm

they have a number of people among them who were sick and in all likelihood had other chronic physical issues. Do you see what He does? Jesus never plays the 'excuse-me-I-was-kind-of-talking-to-my-Heavenly-Father' card or keeps them waiting. The text says '[w]hen he went ashore … he had compassion on them and healed their sick.'

Skip over to Matthew 20. Toward the end of that chapter, Jesus is on the move, taking His disciples out of the city of Jericho, when all of a sudden, He crosses paths with two blind men who are begging by the side of the road (that's basically how you garnered an income in ancient times if you were disabled). Both men cry out for Jesus to have mercy on them, and then they have to repeat themselves because the crowd following Jesus told Him not to bother with them. Instead of listening to the mob, Jesus leans in to the request of the blind men: *'Lord, let our eyes be opened.'* The response? *'And Jesus in pity touched their eyes, and immediately they recovered their sight and followed him.'*

And there is Luke 5, where Jesus breaks social protocol and reaches out and touches a leper, healing his condition instantly. To touch someone with a ghastly skin condition like that was to break a social taboo; one just didn't do that! But Jesus did. Or take a peek at Luke 8, when again Jesus is with His disciples and a large crowd (which is helpful to have eyewitnesses to a miracle!). And we find Jesus squeezed on all sides by a great crowd. Somehow, in the midst of this crush of humanity, a woman totters and stumbles along, a woman who is suffering from an internal blood disorder, a woman who has lost her entire life savings seeking a cure for her disability. And she reaches out in desperation to touch Jesus' robe, and the moment her fingertips touch the fringe of His garment, she's healed! Jesus even commends her warmly and kindly for her faith!

What do these examples have in common that is practical for us today? Well, yes, Jesus healed them all, but let's assume we're not going to have the healing power of the Son of God at our disposal. The common thread in each story is *compassion*.

Jesus **had compassion** on the sick and suffering by the seashore; He touched the blind men's eyes **in pity**; He touches a leper, which is an action designed to demonstrate **compassion**; and He warmly comments on a weak lady's faith, words that have to be drenched in **compassion,** tenderness, and empathy.

That is the first takeaway from Jesus's actions. Likewise, we are to be people of compassion when we come into contact with people who are disabled. Unfortunately, due to awkwardness, anxiety, or even ignorance, nearly two-thirds of all people are uncomfortable talking to or spending time with disabled people.[7] Surely these are fears that must be overcome.

Another reason why engagement with disabled persons is so beneficial and critical is that we can see both our true need for God and how Jesus acts on our behalf. Several years ago, at a conference in West Bromwich, England, Joni Eareckson Tada spoke clearly and happily about this. She told the audience, 'Our Saviour chose to flash His credentials as Messiah through ministry to disabled people … A disability magnifies God's grace … We in our wheelchairs get to prove how great and trustworthy God is.' There is great power in the lives of disabled people, for in what weakness they show, we all get a demonstration of our own weakness and helplessness before God. Only if Jesus intervenes on our behalf in His life, death, and resurrection do we have any hope of falling into the arms of God in faith. We cannot walk to God unless the Holy Spirit empowers us, we cannot see God unless the Spirit opens our

---

7. https://www.newstatesman.com/voices/2014/05/two-thirds-us-are-uncomfortable-talking-disabled-people-we-need-time-money-and-effort

eyes, and we cannot express faith in Christ unless the Holy Spirit moves us to do so.

'Now What?': How Do I Respond?

When we lived in Florida, I saw firsthand how some people can bungle moments around the disabled. I was wheeling my (then) nine-year-old Joshua across the campus of the school where I taught. We passed a group of fourth graders and the sight of Joshua in his wheelchair caught the eye of one of the kids, who promptly blurted out, 'What's wrong with him?' I confess the Holy Spirit was pulling yeoman duty that day, preventing me from making a snarky comment back like, 'Nothing's wrong with him; what's wrong with you?' (Although I'll admit I thought it.) That was, of course, a unique situation. But even people who might willfully and kindly desire to engage those with physical disabilities can struggle with their approach. What then?

First of all, this desire is the right one and people should seek to nurture and develop a passion for coming alongside the physically impaired. It is a testament to who we are as those who bear God's image that we should befriend the disabled. This reminds me of Bill Bennot's quote: 'How we walk with the broken speaks louder than how we sit with the great.'[8] Loving, encouraging, and serving the disabled is a matter of character development, and that means doing so because you *want to*, not out of a grudging sense that you *have to*.

Also, perhaps you have a desire to love people with disabilities well, but you might wonder—once you get into the same room as a person with cerebral palsy, or who has Down's Syndrome, or uses a wheelchair—what are the ground rules? *How should I act in a way that is decent and doesn't offend someone else?*

---

8. See his *Unstoppable Kingdom*.

Well, I'd encourage you to relax. As with spending time with anyone else, just relax and be yourself. Don't try to be someone you're not! Also,

- Know the person's name and express it often.

- Even when referencing a disabled person in conversation with others, speak about them as straightforwardly as possible. Say, 'I spent last evening playing video games with my friend Elise', not 'I was playing video games with my cerebral palsied friend Elise.'

- Speak clearly with people who have cognitive disabilities.

- Allow people with speech impediments as much time as they need to get their words out, and smile proudly that they make the effort.

- When conversing with a person in a wheelchair, squat or bend down and get on their eye level to communicate equality. Don't lean on the wheelchair or grab it, but give them space.

There's more we could say here, but that should be enough to get you started.

'Now What?': We Are Shaped by the Broken

I've been pressing the point throughout this section that we are designed for a purpose. Whether great or small, highly noticed or mostly under the radar, no life is unimportant. Everything we do, to paraphrase Martin Luther, honors the Designer, not just because *what we do* matters, but because *who we are* matters.

Nothing shaped my understanding of this more than the short but beautiful life of our youngest child, Jordan. We desperately tried to save his life on the autumn morning he passed away, but our efforts and those of the paramedics came up short. Moments after the doctors ended the attempts to resuscitate our baby boy, Christi and I held him in the emergency room. I looked down at Jordan, his earthly disability-marked shell with us while his renewed body cavorted and scampered about in heaven. I appraised his light brown hair and stony brown eyes that looked back at us through small slits. What a lovely little child who brought us wonderful memories. His smile could light up a room, and his hugs and kisses reflected the gentle, unquestioned love that God has for His people. We cried and held him some more in silence, until my wife broke the quiet as she kissed Jordan tenderly before saying, 'I know he was with us for only a short time, but I'm still so happy we got to have him.'

That's at the core of everyone's being, whether you live for eighty-four years, eight years and four months, eight months and four days, eighty minutes and four seconds, or eighty-four seconds after conception. Whether you are an Olympic athlete or a child with cystic fibrosis. Who you are matters, and you matter supremely, because you have been designed supremely to matter for as long as you have breath. And even beyond that.

Those who are disabled have a precious platform to shape others with their beautiful and brave daily fights against their challenges. And we who live alongside them have the privilege of being built up and encouraged by their quiet strength. So the question is: Who can encourage you by their determined battle today? Are you willing to admit your life can be deepened and enriched by their presence?

For Your Consideration

- What makes physical disability and how we treat the disabled a <u>moral</u> issue?

- How might you give hope and encouragement to a disabled person who is overwhelmed or in despair about their disability?

- Consider the saying: *How we walk with the broken speaks louder than how we sit with the great.* How would churches, businesses, schools, and individuals be different if they really and consistently lived that out?

- Think back to our chapter on abortion: What would you share with a couple (assuming they are friends of yours) who find out they are pregnant but they also discover through pre-natal testing that their child will likely be significantly disabled. They are advised by others to have an abortion. What do you say and how do you craft your advice to them?

10

Bioethics

IN late 1993, I accompanied several mates to a second-run theatre in suburban St Louis. Desirous for a break from seminary studies, we decided to plunk down a dollar each to see what the big deal was about the film *Jurassic Park*. Anyone who has ever seen that movie, even if they didn't necessarily enjoy the plot, knows it was a significant moment in cinema development, given the cutting-edge computer-generated technology and animatronic elements in visual effects. *Jurassic Park* became the highest-grossing film at the box office that year and—until *Titanic* came along in 1997 and broke the billion-dollar level in ticket sales—it was the highest-grossing film of all time.

But neither the numbers, nor the storyline, nor the visual effects of *Jurassic Park* are what have stayed with me over the years. The seminal moment of the entire film occurs when the main characters are lunching before going out into the park for a guided tour. John Hammond (played by Sir Richard Attenborough) pleads desperately with the scientists he has flown in for observation, eagerly hoping for their endorsement of his work in genetic mutation and cloned dinosaurs. In a firm, no-nonsense rebuke, Dr Ian Malcolm (Jeff Goldblum's character, for those who recall) sternly warns Hammond of the implications of his creation: 'Genetic power is the most awesome force the planet has ever seen, but you wield it like a kid that's found his dad's gun.' Hammond begs off the stinging barb by saying their scientists have done unique things, taking genetics into areas where no one has gone before.

And that's when Malcolm delivers the line of the film. 'Yeah, yeah, but your scientists were so preoccupied with whether or not they could that they didn't stop to think if they should!'

Jurassic Park is no mere scientific thrill ride. In a real sense, it is a picture of our world condensed into two hours on the screen. I don't mean we have cloned dinosaurs running about (you'd know it if we did … just follow the shrieks), but that there is a spirit of the age pressing certain issues in human development and genetics forward at a significant speed, and we need to ask if the pace and actions of this worldview are appropriate. In short, we are talking about the subject of bioethics.

Now, here is the part where I disappoint you. In keeping with the pace and average chapter length of this book, I will not be plumbing the depths of every issue and question that could arise from this. I'm just trying to orient you to study these issues more deeply. There are many resources that can help you go deeper.[1] I'm just trying to get us asking some questions to prod this issue.

For the time being, let's begin with some inquiries. What matters are the primary activities in bioethics? Why does the pursuit of this kind of human advancement matter at all? And what can we do as individuals and groups to intervene when we are able?

---

1. Some great works to get you started include John Wyatt's *Matters of Life and Death, 2nd ed.* (IVP, 2015), Lee Silver's *Remaking Eden* (Ecco, 2007), and Michael Guillen's article 'The Case Against Perfection' in the April 2004 issue of *The Atlantic,* which you can view at https://www.theatlantic.com/magazine/archive/2004/04/the-case-against-perfection/302927/

'What?': Life Becoming Perfected

Previously, we have discussed moral issues like abortion, suicide, and euthanasia, activities which have to do with taking life. The bioethical frontier that concerns us now majors in what my colleague Dr Andrew Shaw calls 'making and faking life.' That horizon contains more than we can adequately describe in a few pages, but for our purposes here, we'll focus on the following categories:

(1) In-vitro fertilization: IVF is a series of procedures designed to assist in the conception of a child. While there are several forms of assisted reproductive technology, IVF is the most well-known one. In IVF, medical professionals will collect mature eggs from a female's ovaries in a laboratory and then fertilize these eggs with male sperm. The IVF procedure may be executed with the couple's gametes (sex cells) or those of a donor.[2] A process of three weeks or longer, IVF is designed as a countermeasure to infertility or certain health problems in the reproductive process.[3] In theory, the procedure can result in a fertilized egg and thus a pregnancy that can lead to the birth of a child. Sometimes, IVF results in multiple blessings of twins, triplets, or more.

(2) Stem cell activity: Mainly for the purposes of discovering cures for longstanding diseases and afflictions, this technology collects *stem cells*, cells from which over two hundred different tissues in the human body originate. Researchers utilize stem cells as a way of seeking cures

---

2. https://www.mayoclinic.org/tests-procedures/in-vitro-fertilization/about/pac-20384716

3. damage to the Fallopian tubes. Again, see the previously noted Mayo Clinic page.

for conditions like Parkinson's disease, autoimmune diseases, cancer, and so on. The stem cells in question come from two pools of collection: from human embryos and from live adults. We'll deal with the ethics of each of these in the next section.

3. Reprogenetics: Often known as embryonic selection, reprogenetics is the process by which couples can go through a process of prenatal diagnosis, testing prenatal tissue in embryos to screen for potential diseases and then selecting the embryos that do not display the afflicted traits.[4] The technology has advanced to the point where doctors can test for single-gene issues, such as Huntingdon's disease.

4. Trans-humanism: Trans-humanism, also known philosophically as post-humanism, offers a radical new vision of humanity that found a new voice in Donna Haraway's *The Cyborg Manifesto* in 1985. She saw the scientific creation of cyborgs as in-between creatures exhibiting human and machine traits. These cyborgs would blur the lines between male and female, physical and non-physical, which in Haraway's view would expand the potential for our freedom.[5] Bioengineered and trans-human activity has periodically made its way into cinematic releases from Hollywood, from 1982's *Blade Runner* to the Best Picture Award-winning *The Shape of Water* in 2018. The key desire of the trans-humanism movement is to position science to enhance human intellect and activity, eventually transforming into new

---

4. https://www.nature.com/scitable/topicpage/embryo-screening-and-the-ethics-of-human-60561

5. This is taken from Michael Plato's *What is Posthumanism?*, published by Davenant Press in early 2019, pp. 7-8.

beings with broadened and amplified potential that goes beyond human capabilities.

'So What?': But at What Price?

I think it's only fair to say that a number of these activities arise from well-meaning motives. Couples who struggle to have children find IVF an option that might be their best chance at conception. A wife who watches her husband's hands shake violently due to his Parkinson's disease hopes for a cure that could be available through stem cells. A mother and father whose first two children died early from severe genetic disorders might want clarity on whether another pregnancy could bring more of the same. And who would not want enhanced capabilities and a better life?

Nor can one simply write off IVF, stem cell research, repro-genetics, or trans-humanism by saying, 'Well, the Bible never says such things are okay. We should let nature be untouched in this regard.' I notice such people may be relatively unbothered by driving around in automobiles (which weren't around in biblical times), or taking ibuprofen for a headache, or by the suburban sprawl of homes and businesses over God's pristine creation. We have to consider how humans were designed to function, as unique creations of God, and if such methods honor or dishonor God in their implementation.

Regarding IVF, there are countless examples of couples who have been able to get pregnant and who cherish their children tremendously. This is definitely a noble result of the procedure. There are some practical matters that people must consider before going down this road, though. IVF is a process that takes a great deal of time and energy. It is also expensive, with significantly high out-of-pocket costs. And the invasive nature of the procedures can occasionally result in physical problems for the mother or baby. There is a slight increase in the chance that the child could be born early and/or with decreased weight. Fertility drugs used to cause ovulation can cause extended pain in the ovaries. And along with the financial stress and strain, the process of IVF can drain the mother's physical and emotional strength. In certain situations, there are also moral disturbances one must consider. What happens to fertilized embryos that are not implanted? Are they cast aside? Used for research purposes? Brent Kunkle notes that destroying fertilized embryos certainly seems to be short-circuiting human life and is the equivalent of killing a 'living, distinct, human being.'[6] Storing embryos also raises concerns about treating human life—even at the smallest stages—as a commodity, a package to be used or forgotten at our convenience. This may not be the concern of couples going through IVF, but it is a potential side-effect of the industry itself.

Stem cell research and development carries a number of questions in its wake. Fertility clinics (where IVF can take place) can donate their left-over embryos for stem cell labor. When researchers take stem cells from these fertilized embryos, their action brings about the destruction of these distinct, human persons.[7] The supporters of embryonic stem cell research promote their activity based on the potential of the cells to multiply and create cures at a more rapid rate, a feature called *pluripotency*. Simply put, some will say that using embryonic stem cells is more efficient with a higher rate of return than adult, non-embryonic stem cells. Yet many roadblocks are showing up on the embryonic side of stem cells. Genetic expression is

---

6. https://www.str.org/blog/moral-factors-take-account-if-youre-considering-ivf

7. The question also arises if there is a moral issue with taking stem cells from an unborn child that has already died. This matter has several layers to it. If the unborn child is stillborn or miscarried, then stem cell work on the body would be without ethical bounds. If the dead baby is the result of abortion, an action which we have dealt with in a preceding chapter, then the stem cells are received via unethical means.

more and more unstable, tumors can manifest themselves, and stem cells can have severe difficulty forming the desired tissue for human need. In fact, as stem cell research has evolved, professionals are discovering that adult and umbilical cord stem cells are displaying greater potency than their embryonic counterparts, thus granting a better chance at discovering cures for major diseases and avoiding ethical land mines.[8]

With reprogenetics, there are significant dilemmas. Couples who can select specific embryos based on their constitution or gender have to ask why they are making these choices. Is it for information, so they know what they might be getting into with a pregnancy or the road of parenthood? Or is it to discriminate, to choose and discard? And if we do that, are we not placing ourselves in the place of God? Is this not deciding there are some worthy of being treasured and others who do not make that cut? What happens if we commit to going down that path? And what about the very nature of parenthood? Doesn't the ability to select the characteristics of one's child make being a parent more consumer-focused than steeped in responsibility for others in your care?

Trans-humanism carries with it an air of mystery; it is the most open-ended direction bioethics can take. And within that lies a certain level of disturbance. We already live in an age of genetic enhancement. The field of agriculture is loaded with examples. New York University School of Medicine was able to engineer a completely new species of yeast using CRISPR technology, and the University of Delft was the site of the 2015 invention of synthetic meat.[9] The question becomes: What happens when we push the limits to create species that can

---

8. https://stemcellresearch.org/wp-content/uploads/2012/11/ASCRPlasticity.pdf

9. *What is Posthumanism?*, pp. 12-14.

'intelligently' interact with humans but are not fully human themselves? This is the boundary that *The Shape of Water* (referred to earlier) pushes against, where human interaction with beings of artificial intelligence can mimic the greatest level of intimacy, leading to trans-species romance. Transhumanism promises to grant us greater freedom and more options for interaction with others. What I fear it reveals is a creeping philosophy that no longer views human beings as unique, special creations in their own ways. Also, how can one be sure such future interaction will 'work' or be beneficial between humans and cyborgs? Ian Malcolm's warning from *Jurassic Park* seems to ring even more true. And on the subject of created dignity, doesn't the creation of trans-human species by humans necessarily show that people are, in fact, a logically higher order beings than what they construct?

'Now What?': Responding Biblically and Constructively

A protest based solely on fear is unattractive and unhelpful. Scripture and reasonable thinking are much more effective. There are some points to consider if we want to make practical, godly headway amongst these issues.

First, we should be willing to challenge any activity within science that objectifies people and treats human beings as disposable commodities. The idea that human beings—born or unborn and of any age—are mere objects whose value is based on what we can perceive it to be flies in the face of common sense and Scripture. As we discussed in the previous 'The Meaning of Life' chapter, *'If life is only worth living if the odds of suffering are greatly decreased, or if the odds of comfort and ability are higher, or if the person "cannot contribute to society", then that betrays an attitude that we can make the call on people deemed less "worthy." And at what point do you draw that line? ... The truth is that we are either designed on purpose—however flawed* and limited our bodily abilities are—or we are not. Our <u>essence</u> is either that of people charged with and infused with dignity, or worthless piles of nothingness.' Psalm 8 implores us to remember that God has formed each human being with the designation of being made

> 'a little lower than the heavenly beings
>   and crowned him with glory and honor.
> You have given him dominion over the works of
> your hands;
>   you have put all things under his feet,
> all sheep and oxen,
>   and also the beasts of the field,
> the birds of the heavens, and the fish of the sea,
>   whatever passes along the paths of the seas'
>
>   (Ps. 8:5-8).

Rubbing shoulders with archangels and being crowned with glory and honor seem to be more than what embryonic stem cell research, reprogenetics, and trans-humanism offer. Thus, in our response to any bioethical matter, we need to make sure that human rights and liberties get our fierce defense.[10]

Another consideration is that we should show compassion and empathy for people who feel they need to opt for these processes. We should not paint IVF or stem cell research, for example, with such a broad brush that we critique people without thinking about their individual situations. I have friends (one former student) who had difficulty in getting pregnant. They wanted children, and it was only through IVF they were able to have that chance. Their primary thought wasn't sacrificing their morals on a bioethical altar; they wanted to have children

---

10. And as we'll discover later, this needs to be apparent in issues such as immigration, just to be consistent.

of their own and love them dearly. Can't we commiserate with them? Doesn't God weep for and show pity upon barren women, as is shown so often in the Bible (Sarah in Genesis 21, Rebekah in Genesis 25, Samson's mother in Judges 13, Hannah in 1 Samuel 1-2, and Elizabeth in Luke 1, to name a few)? Can't we at least understand their hopes and tears? What about the elderly man who loves his wife well even as she can't recognize him because of her Alzheimer's disease? Can you understand why stem cell research in pursuit of that cure would be on his mind and heart?

One other concern we should have is the accessibility of proper medical procedures and innovations to as many as require them. Given the prohibitive cost of some opportunities, so much of the availability of such technology is centered in the geographical and (relatively wealthy) Euro-American Western population. Now, don't get me wrong ... I love where I live. However, when we are able to take advantage of technology to assist in reproduction or combatting rare diseases, while children and adults in the Majority World face starvation and lack of access to clean drinking water, that's an issue of injustice that demands Christian concern and action. Find your voice so that you might '[o]pen your mouth for the mute, for the rights of all who are destitute. Open your mouth, judge righteously, defend the rights of the poor and needy' (Prov. 31:8-9).

Above all, let's look at the bioethical maze before us as an opportunity, not only as a threat. This is a chance for young, emerging Christian thinkers and activists to put a new story before others. Instead of hearing the scientific, reductionist clamor to measure everything, to quantify human achievement, to see humans as one mere species among many, what if we gave people a grander hope than that and lived it out? What if people heard and saw from us a conviction that we are not just self-repeating globs of biology but we are flawed yet glorious representatives of a perfect and gloriously loving God? What if we supported scientific achievement yet loved the needy well? What if we fought for cures yet showed supreme confidence in a future transformed by God and not mere human effort? God has called us to live out a different story, His story, one that is infinitely more exciting and thrilling. What if others caught the beauty of that story in your life?

For Your Consideration

- Out of all the bioethical issues mentioned in this chapter, which one brings about the strongest reaction from you? Why does it make that impact on your thinking and convictions?

- What is the danger in replying to bioethical matters with, 'Well, the Bible never says this is okay.' If you were to be consistent, what else would become problematic in your life?

- Trace how one's fundamental views on the meaning of life (chapter 4) and abortion (chapter 6) play into one's stance toward various bioethical controversies.

- What is a positive, proactive contribution you can make toward this issue, and how would you go about doing that?

PART THREE
RELATIONSHIPS MATTER

WE are the living. We have established that. And how we live and uphold life matters.

And how we forge connections and establish intimacy matters, as well.

Few items get the blood flowing than discussions about sex and sexuality. It's as if we instinctively realize that we are not meant to be alone (echoing God's words early in Scripture), and thus anything that affects our relationships is of prime importance.

What is it about relationships that helps us flourish, we wonder? And what activities bring so much pain to us, and why do they do so? How are men and women different yet equal? Is marriage that necessary? Why does divorce rip apart people's hearts? Is pornography a victimless activity? What's the big deal about homosexuality, same-sex marriage, transgender people, or the alphabet soup of sexual identities?

Those are some of the questions. Turn the page, because looking for the answers can't occur on this one!

11

Gender and Honor

WITHIN a month of each other, the following events happened:

(1) Well-known individuals were hit with the public disgrace of sexual harassment and misconduct charges. These included people such as movie producer Harvey Weinstein (fired from his company and expelled from the Academy of Motion Pictures),[1] Al Franken (resigned from the United States Senate),[2] and judge Roy Moore (lost in a special Senate election in Alabama).[3]

(2) Authorities in Cabarrus County (north of Charlotte), North Carolina informed parents and the press that commercial sex trafficking had infiltrated the female student population of the schools in the county.[4]

---

1. https://www.theguardian.com/film/2017/oct/14/harvey-weinstein-oscars-academy-holds-emergency-meeting

2. https://www.politico.com/story/2017/12/06/gillibrand-calls-on-franken-to-resign-282112

3. https://abcnews.go.com/US/roy-moores-accusers-responses/

4. https://www.independenttribune.com/news/experts-human-trafficking-is-in-cabarrus-county/article

(3)   Male students at my school, when approaching a class-
      room doorway from the opposite direction of a female
      student who was coming to the doorway at the same
      time, overwhelmingly barged through the door and did
      not allow the female to go first. We're talking nineteen
      times out of twenty here.

These are distinct events connected by an underlying issue.
They demonstrate that the uphill struggle for women's respect
and honor can appear noticeably steep. I wish I didn't have to
address this matter, but that day is long overdue.

Celebrities and schools are not the only places that exhibit
diffidence (at best) toward the dignity of females. Last year,
the president of a major seminary (that's a graduate school
dedicated to training people for ministry in the church) was
dismissed. Years ago, the man—a revered leader in his faith
community—had been informed by a young woman that she
had been raped by another student. The president did not report
the allegation to police, discouraged her from doing the same,
and strongly urged her to forgive her assailant. More recently,
the same president had received reports of another assault and
sent an email to the head of campus security. His orders were
to allow him (the president) to meet with the student alone to
'break her down' with no other officials present. This followed
other incidents in which several of his comments regarding
women could only be described as uncharitable at best.[5]

'What?': The Issue Before Us

Stories like these make the news every day. We see the results
of dishonoring women around us, and these narratives should

---

5. https://www.washingtonpost.com/news/acts-of-faith/wp/2018/06/01/
southern-baptist-seminary-drops-bombshell-why-paige-patterson-was-
fired/?utm_term=.bfac8bb20eea

sadden us deeply. The establishment of male and female by God at creation was an intentional act of God, and within that intentional act should flow the treasuring of each gender by the other.

Notice that the first human, Adam, has a powerful shaping role amongst God's creation. He names the animals—or at least the members of the animal kingdom around him at the time—and the creation story clearly points to Adam as above the rest of the stuff that God has constructed. But Adam experiences the harsh truth that he does not have a partner like the animals do, a situation that God speaks to: 'It is not good that the man should be alone; I will make him a helper fit for him' (Gen. 2:18). Think about that! After repeated times of stepping back and looking at the beautiful and developing art gallery of His world, God rhythmically says at various points of creation that 'it is good … it is good … it is very good.' But here, for the first time, as Adam lacks a partner, a mate, a true soulmate, an incarnate antidepressant, God utters for the first time the words 'It is not good.' God is saying the *absence of women will be a detriment to the flourishing of His world*! This is years before Tom Cruise told Renee Zellweger in *Jerry Maguire* that 'You complete me.' And so, God creates Eve after some efficient rib surgery on Adam, who immediately gives an enthusiastic double thumbs-up to his glowing bride.

And the relationship, at its core, is between two people equal in worth and formation in the image of God. The very way that God fashions Eve for Adam reflects this. I love how seventeenth-century commentator Matthew Henry puts it in such a lyrical way, when he refers to Eve's creation out of Adam as one who was '[n]ot made out of his head to rule over him, nor out of his feet to be trampled upon by him, but out of his side to be equal with him, under his arm to be protected, and near his heart to be beloved.'[6]

---

6. Matthew Henry, 'Notes on Genesis 2:21-25', *Commentary on the Whole Bible, vol. 1: Genesis-Deuteronomy*.

This fundamental equality maintains itself even after human-kind fell into sin and rebellion against God. There are many ways in which relations between man and woman might be bruised and vandalized by sin, but the equality of worth in God's eyes is not lost through this cosmic ruin. In fact, the Bible goes to great lengths to display the honor and equality of women throughout its pages. In the Old Testament, while a family's father would take the primary responsibility for the leadership and well-being of his wife and children, the mother had a great deal of authority as well. Carol Meyers points out that in Hebrew society, women 'functioned as the ... chief operating officers of their household. They were hardly oppressed and powerless ... female-male relationships are marked by interdependence or mutual dependence.'[7] Women were expected to be part of the instruction process of their children. Proverbs 1:8's urging that children should 'not forsake your mother's teaching' seems underwhelming except for the fact that Hebrew society was the only one in the ancient Near East literature where mothers were mentioned as teachers.[8]

The New Testament doesn't change things, either. Jesus instructs women directly as His followers (Luke 10:38-42), and several women are mentioned by name for their ministry actions on Jesus' behalf. The first individuals to notice the resurrection of Christ were women, and Mary Magdalene herself was privileged to encounter the risen Lord in the flesh (John 20:1-18).

'So What?': Fault Lines

In spite of the biblical and longstanding equality of females, our world has a checkered history of aligning itself with these

---

7. Carol Meyers, 'Was Ancient Israel a Patriarchal Society?', *Journal of Biblical Literature* 133/1 (2014): pp. 21-22.

8. Bruce Waltke, *An Old Testament Theology: An Exegetical, Canonical, and Thematic Approach* (Grand Rapids: Zondervan, 2007), p. 240.

realities. People, both secular and religious, can undervalue or disdain the giftedness and worth of women. These fault lines appear in a variety of areas.

For one, leadership can be exhibited in domineering and cruel fashion, as God notes in Genesis 3 as the fall into sin means the man can have a tendency to do this.[9] There have been times when men overwhelm and inhibit women rather than humbly displaying godly integrity, character, and grace. This shows up in abusive households. It also can present itself in churches and faith communities where the ideas of women are pitched aside and not even considered. I even know of at least one Christian denomination where women are not allowed to vote in congregational meetings; to me, there's something seriously wrong with that! Therefore, one of the essential parts of treating women well is for men to re-think what godly leadership looks like. In marriage, that means loving your wife 'as Christ loved the church and gave himself up for her' (Eph. 5:25), in a sacrificial way that doesn't utilize brute force. In the workforce, that means having a humble heart and a listening ear to your employees and colleagues.

A further problem comes in that a good measure of what passes for a 'push for women's equality' is not so much about justice but playing with words. This can happen in many places in our communities, but I saw this played out in one of my favorite shows on Britbox, the political satire comedy *Yes, Minister*.[10]

---

9. Genesis 3:16b. One of the shake-outs of the Great Ruin is that men will get leadership wrong. Either they can go passive and let the woman they are partnered with splash with great force over the reservoir of their relationship, or the man can react by giving the woman no opportunity to voice opinions or act meaningfully.

10. From 'Equal Opportunities', the first episode of the third series of *Yes, Minister*, with an original broadcast of 11 November 1982. The show starred Paul Eddington as MP Jim Hacker and Sir Nigel Hawthorne as his Permanent Secretary, Sir Humphrey Appleby. If you ever want to see

Upon realizing that women make up only 4-5 per cent of senior posts in the British civil service (that's the government, for any American readers), Jim Hacker—who heads up the 'Ministry of Administrative Affairs'—proposes that this be raised to at least 25 per cent within the next four years, leading to an eventual 50 per cent. Hacker's permanent secretary, Sir Humphrey Appleby, hems and haws in delay over this, but Hacker stands firm. Yet in a meeting of the permanent secretaries (all male, by the way), all the members agree 'in principle' there should be more women in senior posts, but there are obvious practical problems. The secretary for the Foreign Office says they couldn't appoint women ambassadors to Muslim or Arab nations. In the Home Office, it is suggested, women shouldn't be running prisons or police, because 'they wouldn't want to do it anyway.' For Defence, 'it's clearly a man's world.' And yet, in concluding the meeting, all the men agree that the feeling is 'in principle … we're all in favor of equal rights for the ladies, but there are special problems in individual departments.' With a comic touch, the show makes a serious point: Very often, the affirmation of women's worth and equality can be limited to words rather than meaningful action.

Yet another fault line can exhibit itself from the woman's side. I referred to Genesis 3 before, where God confronts the first humans over their rebellion. The relational train wreck for the woman comes when God tells Eve that '[y]our desire shall be for your husband, and he shall rule over you' (Gen. 3:16b). [This doesn't mean, incidentally, that male headship or leadership is a result of human rebellion, but that it gets vandalized and fractured from what God intended.] Note what occurs within the woman: Her desire will be for her husband. That can mean

---

how government inefficiency and the status quo can produce rib-crushing laughter, this is the show!

that either of two toxic paths could occur. A woman can knuckle under and her desire can be such that she will do anything for her man, even letting him dominate her relationally. Or there's the other path, in which the Hebrew word rendered 'for' could also mean 'against' so the passage would read *your desire shall be against your husband.* In this case, the woman would have no patience with the man being the leader and would instead take the steering wheel out of his hands. To be clear: Neither path is godly or wholesome. A woman is not to be passive and allow the man to dominate or define her. Nor should a woman rise up against her man. There is a muscular tension in which both men and women—those interested in applying the work of Jesus to their relationships, anyway—must place themselves. The woman must follow well as an equal and encourage the man to decisive, godly action. The man must lead humbly with a delight in his woman, seeking to affirm the treasure she is so she might unearth her own giftedness in the relationship.

Thus, there are significant challenges we face in this matter. Practically speaking, what are some first steps we can take to walk along a biblical path in the good life?

'Now What?': Treasuring Women Well

Now, I should warn you that there are some things I won't be unpacking here. For example, Christians might debate about the place of leadership within churches, and if women can serve as elders, deacons, pastors/priests, or bishops. While I have definite opinions and strong conclusions on that matter, this is not the place to bring them up. I want to consider what's within the reach of everyone, male or female, and work out some solutions from that point.

First of all, let's recognize that equal worth in the eyes of God—which both men and women enjoy—does not negate a differentiation of roles in family life or other areas. There are things women are equipped to do better than men, and vice versa. It also means that as you might approach—or already be in the midst of—marriage, you are building a family together and must be willing to take on responsibilities for the bettering of the other. You must also discover how your gifts and talents can help the family flourish, and this means not relegating a duty to another merely because you think it's 'man's work' or 'woman's work.' The husband should never expect to have a wife who remains 'barefoot, pregnant, and in the kitchen', nor should the wife expect the husband to work hard for a paycheck that she can overspend with irresponsibility.

For some other practical steps, let me address both sides separately. First, the ladies:

(1) Ultimately, you get your worth and truest love from God, not another man. If you trust completely that God loves you unconditionally, then it is a safeguard against looking for a man to satisfy your needs of affection.

(2) Never, ever be ashamed of how God has gifted you in your abilities or your intellect. Obviously be humble, but don't publicly lessen who you are because you think that's what a man wants. The right men like women with proper confidence in their minds and talents. Pursue your opportunities in education and the workforce as much as you can. Women have more options now than they've had in the past. Don't spurn your chances and assume you'll be a teen dream prom queen[11] that will get scooped up by some rich man and never have to work again.

(3) Sometimes exhibiting your worth means being willing to push away from someone. If a man doesn't reciprocate

---

11. I think that phrase comes from a sermon on gender roles I once heard from Tim Keller of Redeemer Presbyterian Church in New York City.

your interest, ignore him. If he is physically or verbally abusive, stay away from him (and report him!). If you are (a) of marrying age and (b) in an exclusive relationship with a guy for an extended time and (c) he refuses to ask you to marry him, then leave him, because he will never commit to you.

(4) And another exhibition of your inherent worth as a female is affirming and encouraging a guy when he does something right. Thank him for his kindness, his listening skills, and anything else that truly matters. Be specific. I'll fall on the sword for my gender here: We won't admit it, but males can be very insecure and confused souls, so when we've done the right thing and demonstrated goodness to you, we really like to know it.

Now, for the men:

(1) Make a covenant with yourself to not be a pig. If you're an adolescent, I understand you might believe you have the right to sow your immaturity without consequence. But barging through a doorway and not letting a girl go first? Making filthy jokes about a woman's body? It's stupid, toxic, and unattractive behavior. Grow up and be a man.

(2) I know that we live in a world where every action is under scrutiny and can be misinterpreted. But kindness to women truly affirms their worth; it doesn't denigrate their equality or femininity. Open doors for women. When you and a girl approach an open door at the same time (from the same or opposite directions), let her go first. Make eye contact with ladies when you speak to them.[12] Put down your mobile phone when speaking

---

12. That is, with their eyes. Just making sure.

with them. Offer to give up your seat for them. If they drop something, pick it up for them.[13]

3. If you want to be attractive to females, it has very little to do with looks (thank goodness, because I fell woefully short in that category) and a lot to do with the heart. Do things, even the most menial tasks, for them. This covers much of point 2 above, but when you enter marriage, what makes you attractive to your wife is a willingness to do an armload of stuff around the house. Even if you have limited mechanical skills, you can change out some items (putting in new switchplates on the walls is only a YouTube instructional video away, for example). In our house, I empty the dishwasher, do the laundry, and iron any clothes that need it. No one tells me to do so; I just enjoy doing it![14] Christi handles other things in a manageable division of labor that works for us.

4. And to somewhat repeat point 1 from the ladies, you get your identity and worth from Christ. Follow Jesus, love and obey Him, and that will set your compass. And the right kind of woman will naturally gravitate to a man who exhibits godliness and humble, Christ-like servant leadership. I seriously can't stress that enough.

For Your Consideration

● Which do you think is the more empowering, affirming statement about females: 'Women were created to do

---

13. Gentlemen, you never know: This could be a way of a girl showing her interest in you and gauging yours in return. It could be the start of something special.

14. You read that correctly. There's few things as satisfying as looking down at an empty dishwasher, folded clean clothes, or a crisp shirt. I think I just enjoy seeing order come out of chaos.

anything a man can do'? Or 'Women were created to do everything a man can't do'?

- Note the 'fault lines' in the 'So What?' section. Which of these do you think is the most challenging struggle we face on the issues discussed in this chapter?

- Which of the practical applications (in the 'Now What?' section) do you find most applicable to your life? Why do you say that?

- While we must honor women, statistics demonstrate that the most critical component for a child's sense of social well-being, education, ability to empathize, and live life responsibly is the presence of a father/father figure in the child's life. How do males practically lead well in these situations and also demonstrate tenderness and kindness toward women?

12
Marriage and Cohabitation

W HEN I was fifteen years old, the Sidney Pollack-directed film *Out of Africa* garnered seven Oscars at the Academy Awards, including the designation of Best Picture. Meryl Streep and Robert Redford gave commanding performances as divorcee Karen Blixen and big game hunter Denys Hatton, respectively, and the film centered greatly on their love story. Enraptured by how Denys makes her feel and finding their time apart to be unbearable, Karen desires marriage. The roadblock to matrimony with Denys is, as it were, Denys himself. Though Karen desperately attempts to win him over to the idea of marriage, the fiercely independent Hatton can't (or won't) make the move. For evidence, the following exchange should suffice:

> **Karen:** '*When you go away ... you don't always go on safari, do you? Just to go away.*'
>
> **Denys:** '*It's not meant to hurt you.*'
>
> **Karen:** '*It does.*'
>
> **Denys:** '*I'm with you because I choose to be with you. I don't want to live someone else's idea of how to live. Don't ask me to do that. I don't want to find out one day that I'm at the end of someone else's life.*'

Or this:

Karen: *'What's wrong with marriage anyway?'*

Denys: *'Have you ever seen one you admire?'*

And finally, after Karen presses him once more on the marriage issue, Denys says *'I won't be closer to you and I won't love you "more" because of a piece of paper.'*[1]

Denys betrays a conviction that settles in the hearts of many people, that marriage, though useful for some, is a constricting endeavor to human independence. He also unloads how little he thinks of marriage by viewing it as a paper contract spelling out its aims. Why, he voices, should love be exemplified by that? Perhaps Karen should have been asking, 'Why is Denys so resistant of true commitment?'

This is not to suggest that there is something wrong with you if you are not married or don't want to be married at the present time. However, attitudes about marriage and family are making more subtle maneuvers than Denys Hatton's outright bluster. For instance, in my own country, Americans are remaining single longer. In 2018, the median age for first marriage reached its peak—thirty years of age for men and twenty-eight years for women.[2] Also, the number of cohabiting adults—men and women living with an unmarried partner—rose nearly 30 per cent in one decade, going from fourteen million adults to eighteen million.[3] And repeat unions are on the rise. Among adults who are presently married, nearly a quarter of them

---

1. A number of these quotes can be garnered from a cursory viewing of the film or by getting a representative list of quotes at https://www.imdb.com/title/tt0089755/quotes/?tab=qt&ref_=tt_trv_qu

2. https://www.pewresearch.org/fact-tank/2019/02/13/8-facts-about-love-and-marriage/

3. https://www.pewresearch.org/fact-tank/2017/04/06/number-of-u-s-adults-cohabiting-with-a-partner-continues-to-rise-especially-among-those-50-and-older/

have been married before, compared to only 13 per cent at the beginning of the 1960s.[4]

The importance of these issues, marriage on the one hand and cohabitation on the other, demands that we understand them well. If God has set out what the good life is like, how do these paths fit in?

'What?': Defining Each Journey

If we take Scripture and common sense seriously, we find that marriage is a relationship blessed by God and was in existence (Gen. 1) before sin even marred the universe (Gen. 3). But *why* does God bless marriage to be the way it is? Well, there is a **procreational** reason: to build a family through the bringing forth of children. God does say to be fruitful and multiply and fill the earth (Gen. 1:28).[5]

Also, God points out a **relational** component when it became apparent Adam didn't have a creature that was like him. In the midst of everything good about creation, God states that '[I]t is *not good* that the man should be alone; I will make him a helper fit for him.' That is, the King of the universe was going to craft a being who would complete and fill in the gaps for the male in the deepest, most intimate, and most fulfilling ways. This is why, during a wedding ceremony, our ears might be especially attuned to the vows between husband and wife, to be *companions* in sickness and in health, in plenty and in want, for richer or for poorer.

---

4. https://www.pewsocialtrends.org/2014/11/14/four-in-ten-couples-are-saying-i-do-again/. It's noteworthy that men are more apt to get remarried than women.

5. While it's true that children are a blessing from God (Ps. 127:3-5: 'Behold, children are a heritage from the LORD, the fruit of the womb a reward. Like arrows in the hand of a warrior are the children of one's youth. Blessed is the man who fills his quiver with them!'), the inability to conceive should never be viewed as the result of God's displeasure. Infertile couples require compassion and love rather than low-grade disdain.

In addition, the marriage is intended for **sexual** commitment that displays the selfless and devoted love between husband and wife, the essence of what Genesis 2:24 calls 'one flesh.'

In fact, Genesis 2:24 is where we get the clearest biblical expression of marriage in which the procreational, relational, and sexual intents might be realized. In short, marriage exists as:

(a) An exclusive male-female bond (*'A man ... to his wife'*).

(b) The result of an undisguised, clear event. (*'leave his father and his mother'* ... You are marking going from one primary relationship to another).

(c) Total, all-in commitment (*'shall hold fast to his wife'*).

(d) The arena in which sexual union is fruitfully celebrated and enjoyed (*'they shall become one flesh'*).

Cohabitation—living together in relationship without getting married—seeks to capture the essence and benefits of marriage without cementing it with solemn promises. As shown earlier, social attitudes and actions display more open-ness to cohabitation. There can be several reasons for this. Some adults do not want to be legally married and desire to live together for the enjoyment and the meeting of personal needs. Some might come from dysfunctional families and wish not to repeat the mistakes of their parents' marriages. Others might have an eye on marriage in the future but want to try cohabitation as a test case, a practice run before the 'big game' of marriage. Even some Christian thinkers grant allowances for this. John Sentamu, the Church of England's Archbishop of York, affirms and blesses couples who wish to cohabit, saying that many 'wish to test the milk before they buy the cow.'[6]

---

6. https://www.telegraph.co.uk/news/uknews/royal-wedding/8481736/ Royal-wedding-Archbishop-backs-William-and-Kates-decision-to-live-together-before-marriage.html.

Many people who cohabit believe they are doing so for noble reasons. However, cohabitation cannot be placed on the same level as marriage, mainly due to the lack of both a formal establishment of the relationship and a total commitment. We will return to these matters in the next section.

'So What?': Why Do These Issues Matter?

In light of what seems to be waning enthusiasm for the idea of marriage, why does it matter? What makes marriage so worthy of defense?

First of all, marriage is important because *it is the crucible in which love expresses the highest level of absolute durability.* Loyalty and love can come shining through in many relationships, including friendship and dating. But it is in a committed marriage that the grittiness of love is tested. When a wife reveals something to her husband about a past trauma, they can lean into each other and promise that their commitment to one another won't waver. When a husband and wife determine to be frank and forthright in their disagreements but loving and respectful in how they communicate their words, their children receive a model for how to love others through difficult times. And the children learn a valuable lesson: The key to life is not avoiding hardship, but loving others well through their trials.

This isn't always flashy. Marriage isn't an unbroken chain of days where passion and excitement remain at a fever pitch. Sometimes it's all one can do to keep trudging on. But at its core, love is not an emotion. I'm not saying there aren't emotions and joys connected with love; of course, there are. I'm saying that deep down, when all the layers are stripped away, love is a choice. Every day you will yourself to love your spouse whether it is easy or difficult.

Marriage also serves a social purpose because *it is a catalyst for greater social cohesion and the common good.* Faithful, monogamous marriages can serve as a stable bedrock that can uphold people groups. Even secular researchers notice these implications. A triad of writers from the Royal Society noted that a greater prevalence of committed, faithful marriages between one husband and one wife brings an array of positive results, such as reduced crime rates of rape, murder, assault, robbery, and fraud (likely due to the loving discipline and stability of said families). They also note that monogamous marriages have the effect of changing male priorities from seeking other women to focusing efforts on the family and children. This mindset 'increases saving, child investment, and economic productivity' and 'normative monogamy reduces intra-household conflict, leading to lower rates of child neglect, abuse, accidental death, and homicide.'[7] By affixing oneself to promises and vows that dedicate one to the good of the other person, it should not surprise us that societies with many committed, faithful marriages would evidence more altruism and a higher view of the common good.

Marriage also *exemplifies the discipline and proper passion of sexual union*. Please understand I'm not limiting this to a 'don't have sex if you're unmarried' slogan! You might think the traditional Christian teaching on sex squelches one's fun; in fact, Scripture preserves it. There is a reason why God says that it is after marriage that the husband and wife can now become 'one flesh' or why the writer of Hebrews says 'let the marriage bed be undefiled, for God will judge the sexually immoral and adulterous' (Heb. 13:4).

There are several reasons for this, but I'd offer that one key truth is that God has wired our physical and emotional DNA for monogamy and faithfulness because that is what gets at who we were meant to be. And when we try to re-wire the system or change the ingredients of life, we run into disaster.

---

7. https://royalsocietypublishing.org/doi/full/10.1098/rstb.2011.0290

As a way to illustrate this, imagine you're baking a cake. Because you want that cake to be moist and delicious, you make it according to plan, whether that be the directions on a box of Pillsbury Devil's Food cake mix or Aunt Patty's lemon pound cake. That, friends, would exemplify a proper approach to life and sexual activity as God intended. But what happens if you happen to add three tablespoons more water than needed (yes, I'm making added water the equivalent of sexual experiences before or outside of marriage ... just go along with the analogy)? Well, that cake might still hold, but it'd be a little more runny than normal. Not really what you want. And what if you add another one-fourth of a cup? It gets gushier still. And if you keep adding water (=additional sexual non-marital experiences), the cake *ceases to be a cake!* You just have a river of batter that is beyond useless. Laugh if you wish, but if we carry the analogy over to sex and marriage, then maybe we see the danger and difficulty in veering away from the way God has created us. Not to mention what other practical issues might arise, whether they be unintended pregnancy or sexually transmitted diseases.[8]

As mentioned before, couples who cohabit might seek a situation that is a practice run in case the relationship continues on toward marriage. Some might even call cohabitation 'marriage by another name.' However, as one can see, placing marriage and cohabitation side-by-side reveals that the latter falls woefully short of the former.

---

8. By the way, some people might maintain one can participate in oral sex instead of sexual intercourse and this will be 'safe sex' and one can technically remain a virgin. Whatever they might say, oral sex isn't safe. Any sexually transmitted disease you can contract from sexual intercourse, you can contract from oral sex. And the number of STDs continues to increase, at least in America, at a staggering rate. Take twenty minutes and view the short film *The Rules Have Changed* at https://www.youtube.com/watch?v=9CjmUReV_jU&list=PLKHGbtP0kvJIyheyCC-lzmg_UR9ZA28Ue

Marriage	**Cohabitation**
Exclusive male-female bond	Male-female bond
Inaugurated by public event	No public beginning
Total, all-in commitment	No avowed commitment
Sexual union fruitfully celebrated and enjoyed	Sexual union enjoyed

While there's no doubt that both relationships involve a male and female, and sex can and does take place in both environments, the lack of public profession and commitment reveals significant fault lines about cohabitation.

Whereas marriage begins with a definitive event that leads to a noticeable relationship, cohabitation does not demarcate the pre- and post-relationship identity of the participants, and the relationship is essentially private in nature. Without the presence of specific spoken vows that spell out the determination of the partners (as in marriage), the commitment level of either cohabitant might well be imbalanced from the other. Without a public statement to go all-in on seeking the welfare of the other above oneself, there is no reason to believe one partner will always be there for the other.[9]

The lack of commitment also brings on other ramifications. Without a solid level of trust in the other, emotional and psychological difficulties can follow. This is why cohabiting relationships are nearly twice as likely to break up as married couples.[10] It might explain why cohabiting individuals are anywhere from 30 per cent more to twice as likely to exhibit major depression, anxiety, substance or alcohol abuse, and cohabiting

---

9. Christopher Ash, *Marriage: Sex in the Service of God* (Leicester: IVP, 2003), p. 222.

10. From the 2017 World Family Map, accessed at http://worldfamilymap. ifstudies.org/2017/files/WFM-2017-FullReport.pdf

fathers are 260 per cent more likely to inflict violence upon their partner.[11] It throws light on the fact that even when cohabitation does lead to a marriage commitment in a relational rent-to-own fashion, the living-together-turned-marriage, once it passes the first year of matrimony, tends to fracture much more often than couples who marry without cohabitation.

In short, the evidence is overwhelming even if one does not accept the authority of Scripture: cohabitation is less likely to unleash marital health and success. In fact, just the opposite is true.

'Now What'?: Preparing for the Journey

If you are considering that marriage might be in your future, what are some matters within your control? Maybe you're in your teens and you think marriage is at least a decade away; perhaps you are in the workforce but desire to get married and have a family. What are some steps you can take now?

First, your actions now prepare you for possible marriage later. You don't wait to mature. Choose to cultivate virtue and wisdom now. Think about what marriage would involve, namely that you are seeking the good of another before your own needs for the rest of your life. Would people say that about you now in your present friendships and relationships? If someone asked those who know you, 'Do you experience loyalty/acceptance/honesty from (your name)?', what would your acquaintances say in response?

Secondly, keep the promises you make with a devout sense of responsibility. Be timely in keeping your appointments. If you tell someone you will do X for them, don't switch things around and do Y instead. This is especially critical for young men. Every year in my Biblical Ethics class, I spend some time asking my students what they look for in a potential spouse.

---

11. https://www.ncbi.nlm.nih.gov/pmc/articles/PMC1586128/

When I get feedback from my female students, the overwhelming top answers are 'loyal' and 'dependable.' Throughout life, you'll be faced with doing things because you simply must be responsible in getting them done, not because it's convenient to you. Trust me, the opposite sex is watching.

Moreover, make sure your actions show you treasure others. We've been through some of these matters in the previous chapter on gender and honor, but some things bear repeating. Young men, act with honor. Open doors for females, give up your seat for them, and so on. Ladies, be gracious and appreciative towards young men. These are small items but they should not be overlooked as you are building habits that need to last a lifetime.

Finally, your highest expectations need to be directed at yourself. Yes, it makes all the sense in the world to ask, 'What sort of qualities am I looking for in a future husband or wife?' It's an essential question, but it does not rank at number one. To pine away for whoever might be your soulmate is a stride that wanders off the track.[12] Your primary concern is not what kind of person you should marry. The goal at the top of your list of goals is *to be intentional about the sort of person that you are becoming.* You have a great measure of control in that area. Are you seeking someone who is humble, trustworthy, responsible, and Christ-like? Those are proper expectations. But more importantly, are you seeking to develop those virtues within yourself by the power of the Holy Spirit? Marriage requires you to care about your spouse, but the road to it begins with opening yourself up to what God can do in you.

---

12. And for the record, I don't believe in soulmates. Yes, there's a sense in which you like to 'click' with your spouse, but the truth is that marriage is worthwhile, demanding work, and the marriages that are the most vibrant are the ones in which both husband and wife refuse to quit.

For Your Consideration

- What do you think is the key reason why the average age of first marriages is at its highest level and the number of cohabitations is rising?

- 'At its core, love is not an emotion … love is a choice.' Do you agree with this statement? (Be careful to note the words 'at its core'!) How does God's love for His people demonstrate what true love is?

- What do you think is the best of the reasons for marriage?

- Suppose you know a couple who lived together for three years, then got married. They have been married for eight years, have two children, and things seem to be fine. They say this is proof that cohabitation works. How might you respond to that?

13

Divorce

SEVERAL years ago, *The Guardian* printed some anecdotes from readers about the break-ups of their marriages. To say the stories were wide-ranging would understate things hugely. Recollections ran the spectrum from celebratory to matter-of-fact to heartbreaking.

One reader, a middle-aged Irish woman named Enda, practically exulted. *'While I was totally knocked sideways by my husband's unexpected departure, I came to realise that the situation presented an opportunity for me to focus on me and my own dreams. I moved back to Ireland from the UK, opened my chocolate business here, bought a house in the country, and I've never been happier ... All my dramas are my own, not his. All my successes are my own, not his. All my happiness is my own, not his. My divorce has allowed me to arrive in my own life – and stay here comfortably with a smile on my face and a sense of gratefulness for my health, my happiness and my dream.'*

Another divorcee, American-born Theresa, was more straight-forward. *'We mailed out a "divorce announcement" card. The cover read, "To let you know that we have a new life apart ..." The picture was of two ships, one named "me", the other "you", traveling in different directions with a breaching whale between the two. The back of the card read, "What we call the beginning is often the end.*

And to make an end is to make a beginning. The end is where we start from." Reception to the card was mixed.'

And then came the sad experience of a young British woman who wished to remain anonymous: *'I got divorced earlier this year after two years of marriage. For me, it came really out of the blue. My husband came home one night and told me that he had fallen in love with someone else; when I asked him if our marriage was over, he said, "Yes." And that was it. My parents came and picked me up and took me home. He moved in with her one week later. Finding out he had been unfaithful was a very surreal moment. He was the last person you'd expect to do that, and it sent shockwaves through our family …'*[1]

Whatever can be said about divorce, it's true that no two stories are alike. But no matter what, there is a common element at play: Divorce is not the way life was intended to be.

'What?': From Anecdotes to Pervasive Problem

Divorce is one of those issues that hits close to home. If your family hasn't been marked by it, you at least know someone who has endured it. Yes, there might be a number of marriages that were fraught with severe difficulties from the beginning, and friends and observers might believe the moment of divorce was an eventuality waiting to happen. But there are also marriages that appear—on the surface, at least—to be solid and determined unions, and when they fracture, we're left wondering how that happened. Several of my friends have endured the breakups of their marriages, going down a road they tried desperately to prevent but were unable to do so, and their stories left me in tears along with them.

While there are marriages that fracture and divorce is a sad, necessary remedy in rare circumstances, the truth is we are

---

1. https://www.theguardian.com/lifeandstyle/2016/oct/13/readers-stories-of-divorce

living in an age where people opt out of marriage simply due to lack of satisfaction or the nebulous terminology of 'irreconcilable differences.' The legal catch-all term for this is 'no-fault' divorce, in which husband and wife can end the marriage (1) without either member being guilty of having broken their marriage vows and (2) where neither partner believes the relationship can or should go on. While Russia was the first modern nation to institute no-fault divorce after the October Revolution of 1917,[2] the United States of America features no-fault divorce in every one of its fifty states plus the District of Columbia.[3] And while the United Kingdom has held out for some time, it appears that Parliament will be passing legislation in favor of no-fault divorce.[4]

'What?': The Biblical Desire for Lifelong Marriage

While social tidal waves must be noted, if we are taking the Bible seriously, we should take a look at what it says about divorce. And while it speaks sparingly but clearly about divorce, Scripture says a great deal about the permanence of marriage. Some of these details we covered in the last chapter, but it helps to take a fresh look here.[5]

---

2. See https://www.theatlantic.com/magazine/archive/1926/07/the-russian-effort-to-abolish-marriage/306295/. The Bolshevik movement hated the family unit and believed its abolishment would strengthen the state, which of course was the unquestioned institution of the Communist nation; hence, widespread divorce was the key, leading to exploited women and shelterless children.

3. This trend began in 1969, when California became the first state to pass no-fault divorce into law, under the governorship of lauded conservative and future president Ronald Reagan.

4. https://www.theguardian.com/law/2019/apr/09/no-fault-divorce-law-coming-as-soon-as-parliamentary-time-allows. David Gauke, Secretary for Justice, said 'the outdated law creates or increases conflict between divorcing couples. So I have listened to calls for reform and firmly believe now is the time to end this unnecessary blame game for good.'

5. A number of these findings are drawn from the work of Dr David C. Jones, one of my systematic theology professors from my seminary days. These

First, God's intent is that marriage between man and wife last until one partner dies. Genesis 2:24 clearly states that a man should 'hold fast' to his wife (100 per cent faithful commitment) and become 'one flesh' with her (sexual purity within the husband-wife relationship).

As time went on in a sin-wrecked world, there were times a marriage might be so broken by infidelity that it might need to end. Under Moses' leadership, Deuteronomy 24:1-4 shows us that the only way divorce could happen is if there was 'indecency.'[6] While this word seems general and hard to pin its meaning down, it's helpful to consider what other passages in Scripture might do to clarify it. What we do know is that, in closing out the Old Testament, God is so irate over His people's indiscriminate tendency to faithlessly quit on their marriages that He points out how this is a grievous failure to love one's spouse (Mal. 2:16) and this failure brings about God's hatred.

In the New Testament, we get some clarification from Jesus about what the 'indecency' of Deuteronomy 24 might be. Referencing the law of Moses in Matthew 5:31-32, Jesus says that 'everyone who divorces his wife, except on the ground of sexual immorality, makes her commit adultery.' The Greek word used for 'sexual immorality' which Jesus appears to be equivocating with Moses' 'indecency' is *porneia*, from which we get the word *pornography*. The word was used in a wider sense than the adultery that involved at least one married person; *porneia* is a broad term that includes all wrongful and

---

matters can be pulled from his book *Biblical Christian Ethics* and from his 'Divorce and Remarriage' lecture at Covenant Seminary in 2011: https://www.academia.edu/27008047/Divorce_and_Remarriage_Lecture

6. This passage spends more time on the after-effect of the divorce and potential re-marriages. While re-marriage is a serious matter and needs careful and Biblical consideration, it is not my intent in this chapter to deal with that issue. Dr Jones has done better work than I can in *Biblical Christian Ethics*.

immoral sexual activity. Activities under this banner would include sexually immoral actions like adultery, homosexuality, incest, prostitution, pornography, and others.[7]

Yet this is Jesus dealing with a qualified exception, a marriage-devastating sin. Overall, Jesus' intent is not to quibble about what could give someone the divorce option, but rather Jesus' desire is to defend the permanence of marriage. In Mark 10:7-9, Jesus patiently goes back to the Genesis statement on marriage as the way things were supposed to be, pointing out the husband and wife are no longer 'me and her' or 'me and him', but rather are 'us'; in short, 'the two shall become one flesh.' Jesus drives the point home with the divine claim that this is a lifelong, permanent relationship: 'What therefore God has joined together, let not man separate' (Mark 10:9). Husband and wife are bound to one another as long as they both are alive (Rom. 7:2, 1 Cor. 7:39), and Paul also admonishes the worshipers in the church at Corinth to not give up, but rather dig in and work to transform your existing marriages! (1 Cor. 7:10-11).[8]

'So What?': Why Does Divorce Matter?

Some people, like our first writer at the start of this chapter, believe that divorce 'works things out' and empowers them for

---

7. https://www.samstorms.com/enjoying-god-blog/post/the-problem-of--porneia-

8. Paul does give one other possibility for divorce, and this is for desertion. His specific example comes in 1 Corinthians 7:12-16. The situation might arise where two non-believers get married, and in the course of their marriage, one partner becomes a Christian believer. Paul seems to say that the believing spouse should respect the decision of the unbeliever. If the unbeliever says, 'You know, I love you, but I'm not getting this Jesus stuff you're into, so it might be best if we go our separate ways', then the couple is free to divorce. But if the unbeliever wants the other to remain in the marriage, the marriage should go on. Paul even says, 'You never know how God might be using your marriage, your being on scene with an unbeliever, to draw them into God's kingdom!' And this can be especially critical if there are children involved.

a more fulfilling life. But the easier accessibility to divorce more often than not leads to more trying circumstances than what Enda described.

First of all, we should be concerned about this easier accessibility of no-fault divorce because of how it re-pictures marriage. Instead of marriage being a covenant between husband and wife that creates a sacred arena of life-giving and sacrificial love and commitment, divorce-on-demand turns the concept of marriage into a matter of self-fulfillment. Therefore, 'if my needs aren't being met, I should get out of a situation that is not meeting them.' The direction of energy within the marriage reverses flow: When our expectations are not met, we say that the marriage is not 'working' for us, when in fact *we* are the ones who should be working at our commitment to the marriage.

Divorce-on-demand can also re-position how we tend to face disappointments and difficulties. No one should presume that marriage will create an environment of placid journeys and complete agreement (remember the fall into human sin is a real thing); husband and wife will disappoint one another and let one another down (one hopes this is only occasionally), and marriage—like any relationship—with have its high points and low ones, its peaks and valleys, its joys and tragedies. Marriage is not to be a disposable commodity to be thrown away when life's challenges get to a certain level. Marriage is the proper context in which trust and patience should be increasingly noticeable reactions whenever hardships manifest themselves. The first response of a husband or wife during a marriage trial should not be 'Why isn't he/she seeing it my way?' or even 'How can I get some relief from this trial?', but rather 'How can I show godly patience through this while showing my spouse that I trust him/her?'

Being too trigger-happy about divorce can also create trust issues for others impacted by the marriage breakdown, and the victims who bear the primary brunt of this are children. Sometimes they are helpless bystanders who feel powerless to make positive change; even worse, at other times parents openly or subtly blame their children for family tension. Worse still, as the marriage fully breaks down, some parents use their children for emotional leverage and play favorites in the process of blaming the other spouse. Whatever the 'broken home' story might be for any one child, the result can often be residual pain that shows up in other relationships. This can lead to a reticence to forge friendships or dating relationships, or it can evidence itself in the still, small voice in the back of one's mind that says *'No bond is permanent; there's no reason to expect otherwise; if my own parents couldn't stay together, what realistic chance do I have?'*

This issue is also critical because society has ways of pushing back against healthy marriages, and this is especially glaring in the United States. Child support (post-divorce payments made for the financial care of children from one party to the one who has primary custody of the children) is a *federal matching grant program*. This means that state and local governments, who are the primary one judging child support cases, must spend money on this matter in order to receive federal funding. For every dollar *of administrative costs* that a state or local government spends on implementing the child support program, it receives 66 cents from the national government in Washington, D.C.[9] When it comes to payments and enforcement of child support, though, the federal government provides the majority of the funding.[10] As with any money trail, so much of this is not in

---

9. https://www.acf.hhs.gov/css/ocsedatablog/2017/05/child-support-program-funding-2008-2016

10. http://www.ncsl.org/research/human-services/child-support-adminstration.aspx

the best interest of strong, healthy marriages. The system is set up to fund the breakdown of marriages and to fund situations that represent relational failures. I am not saying we shouldn't have child support, but when a river of money is flowing into a program that incentivizes divorce, one wonders where our society's priorities lie.

'Now What?': Where Do We Go From Here?

In thinking through some practical solutions, we do have to admit there are some times in which divorce is tragically necessary. No, I don't believe the divorce rate should be as high as it is presently,[11] but there are times when infidelity in a marriage has become consistent and so ingrained that one of the partners has no intent of stopping, and in those situations, it would be permissible for divorce to occur. These scenarios would include willful, ongoing, unrepentant lifestyles of adultery, homosexuality, incest, pornography addiction, deliberate desertion, and marital abuse (whether physical, verbal, or sexual).[12] These are brutal, savage behaviors that wickedly impale the very heart of the one-flesh relationship to which God calls husband and wife.

Now, in thinking about a positive direction, I would say there is a great need for careful, biblical instruction about what

---

11. By the way, be especially wary of how some groups calculate the divorce rate among nations. Some will calculate it based on the number of divorces out of every one thousand inhabitants, as the United Nations does. However, this can be misleading as not every one of those inhabitants is getting married. Other groups will take the rate as divorces in a ratio to all marriages, but even this takes some guesswork. Only 41 per cent of all first marriages end in divorce, while 73 per cent of all third marriages end in divorce, so the subsequent attempts at matrimony are driving the overall rate higher. For more, see https://www.wf-lawyers.com/divorce-statistics-and-facts/

12. https://www.christianitytoday.com/women/2016/april/when-does-bible-allow-divorce.html

marriage is in all its glory, hope, and expectation. We need to inform people's minds and stir their hearts to see that marriage is not like co-signing a mortgage on a house, but that it is a God-blessed, Christ-centered, and Holy Spirit-driven life journey of exclusive commitment between husband and wife. To deal with the issue of divorce without addressing the good and wonder of marriage is to miss the point.

We also need to think about how we are preparing ourselves for marriage and for any level of serious commitment. Yes, we can learn from the examples of other, more seasoned couples or read books or online articles on the subject. But in truth, we can also find many opportunities in everyday life to slog on with determination, and if we scale these hills, we will likely find higher mountains (like marriage) more manageable later in life.

Let me share a story that might sound strange, but it's important to me. When I was in the fifth grade at a private school in Mississippi, I played elementary school football (American football, not association football/ soccer). I was a rather chunky tyke, with little raw athletic talent and I would wear out fairly easily. One day, my father and I rode home after practice and I poured out my heart about how difficult football was. I was always tired, I was double-blocked on the front line, and I wasn't playing but a couple of minutes a game as a substitute. Very wisely and quietly, my father said something like this: 'Well, all that might be true, but I think you'll find it important to keep at it and not quit football. It might be hard, but if it wasn't difficult, you might not find it worth doing.' I don't know if that convinced me in the moment, but I never quit the team. In fact, Dad said the best thing about that season wasn't the playing time I got or the contribution I made, but, according to him, 'I'm proud that you stuck it out.' It was then I realized in my ten-year-old mind that being faithful in the small stuff gave you a better chance at being devoted to much more important things. Like marriage.

And that's not to say it's okay to look down on those who come out of failed marriages. Yes, we contribute our shortcomings and sins to every relationship, but it is true that there are spouses that are especially wounded by the violations of their partners. One of my connections on Twitter mentioned that he has eighteen friends who were completely faithful to their spouses, but their spouses violated their trust through adultery, addictions, abuse, or abandonment (I mean, they just walked out and left the husband with the kids and didn't think twice). For all they tried, there could be no reconciliation. Victims such as these need a safe zone where they can land. They desperately require relationships and friendships in which they can vent their sadness and receive comfort, and where they can receive practical help when single parenthood runs into choppy waters. They desire a listening ear when they find it hard to forgive their ex-spouse, and they crave empathy when they are worried about their future and potential romances. It's one thing to know what the Bible would say about marriage and divorce, but it's especially life-giving to ask God for a humble heart so that we might position ourselves to accept those who have been viciously rejected by others. And that is where the gospel of Jesus should motivate us the most. Victims of divorce can often feel the most unworthy and unlovable. We should realize that outside of the gracious reach of God's arm, we were like that at one point, as well.

For Your Consideration

- Of the three reactions to divorce at the start of the chapter, which do you think is the most common for people affected by a divorce? What's your reason for saying that?

- In your opinion, what is the most common reason why people end their marriages?

- What do you believe are the essential ingredients for a healthy marriage that can weather difficult storms of life?

- In Luke 16:10, Jesus says that '[o]ne who is faithful in a very little is also faithful in much.' Although He primarily talks about money there, it seems reasonable that being diligent in smaller matters of life can bode well for building a commitment level for more daunting tasks. What are some of those 'smaller matters' of your life now that you need to be faithful and devoted, so you can construct a consistent pattern of commitment to more serious situations?

14

Pornography

IMAGINE you walk into the kitchen of your home, intent on raiding the refrigerator for food and drink. There, at the counter, is a donkey standing on its hind legs, wearing a polo shirt and skinny jeans and whipping cream into stiffness for a lime and coconut meringue pie. The donkey looks up and says, 'Oh, hi! If you're looking for ginger ale, we probably need to put that on the grocery list. I'm just finishing off this pie for dessert tonight.'

Don't pretend. You'd be shocked to the point of thinking you were in some dream (and wondering what you'd ingested to cause such a vision). An experience like that would be mesmerizing and unique. But imagine how you'd respond if the donkey showed up regularly, making desserts and the occasional entire meal. You'd get used to it, and it would cease to dazzle or excite you anymore. To recreate the same excitement, you'd have to have an experience that went beyond that.

Although what I've described is (ideally) a completely un-likely scenario, this is exactly what another experience can do to you with deadly effect. That explosive habit is *pornography*.

'What?': Defining the Problem of Pornography
In 1964, during a case before the U.S. Supreme Court dealing with pornography and obscenity laws, Judge Potter Stewart admitted

it was practically impossible to define what pornography was and it took an individual reaction to clarify the issue. 'I know it when I see it,' said Stewart in a display of candor, and that became the default mode for years to come.[1]

But surely we can attempt a definition. This may be a long-winded try, and you're free to disagree with me, but I would qualify pornography as cinema rooted in the adult film industry, magazines that display nudity for the purpose of sexual excitement, XXX web sites, online chat rooms designed for filthy sexual conversation and messaging, trashy romance novels (which tend to be badly written literature anyway), sexting of nude selfies or titillating body parts on one's phone, the overwhelming portions of nudity in mainstream films, and a lot of other stuff we don't have room for here – like the entire *Fifty Shades* book and film franchise.

That definition might be little help beyond Stewart's famous edict, but what is significantly daunting is the attitude many have toward viewing porn. In the 1950s, no stores even sold what is commonly called soft-core pornography like *Playboy, Penthouse,* and *Hustler* magazines. In the next decade, *Playboy* was sold behind the counter, followed by *Penthouse* in the next decade. During the 1980s, porn was sold in sealed clear wrapped packaging in bookstores, and with the cosmic reach of the Internet's cyber-tentacles, people now have access to online porn.

Along with society's relaxed access, young people today are taking a more blasé view of pornography. A 2016 Barna Group study probed these thoughts by asking what conversations about pornography are like. The findings showed that 89 per cent of young people and 95 per cent of young adults talk about porn 'in a neutral, accepting, or encouraging way.' An

---

1. https://blogs.wsj.com/law/2007/09/27/the-origins-of-justice-stewarts-i-know-it-when-i-see-it/

additional question asked teens to rate a variety of activities based on how 'morally wrong' they seemed to be. The results showed that ethical quandaries about porn are far down the list. While 56 per cent of teens declared that 'not recycling is usually or always wrong', only 32 per cent said the same thing about viewing pornography.[2]

Just to recap that last statement, nearly double the amount of teens who decry porn are troubled about recycling. And recycling is a good thing (we do have a chapter in this book on ecology and earth stewardship), but what do we make of living in a world inhabited by the above numbers?

'So What?': The Dangers of Being Porn-Again

Why is pornography harmful, you ask? Several reasons for each gender.

For guys, first and foremost, Scripture directs you to faithfulness to your wives. Proverbs 5:16-19a declares the following:

> *Drink water from your own cistern, flowing water from*
> *your own well.*
> *Should your springs be scattered abroad, streams of*
> *water in the streets?*
> *Let them be for yourself alone, and not for strangers*
> *with you.*
> *Let your fountain be blessed, and rejoice in the wife of*
> *your youth, a lovely deer, a graceful doe.*

And Hebrews 13:4 reminds us to

> *[l]et marriage be held in honor among all, and let the marriage*
> *bed be undefiled, for God will judge the sexually immoral and*
> *adulterous.*

---

2. From https://www.barna.com/research/porn-in-the-digital-age-new-research-reveals-10-trends/

There is a life, a journey, an adventure that thrills God as you participate fully in it. On this expedition, you have every opportunity to unearth the treasure of passionate and romantic desire with your spouse for the remainder of your lives together. There is every chance you can know the fullness of such phrases as 'your name is oil poured out' (Song 1:3) and 'you have captivated my heart' (4:9). Did you read that? *Every chance.* But like all of God's gifts, we have the tragic possibility to use our freedom for harm. Grace must properly root itself in holiness, and this takes Spirit-led intentional pursuit of what is good, noble, and lovely because that is God's all-wise proper fit for our spiritual, physical, and emotional DNA.

Forget the excuse that you may not be married yet. You are called to be faithful to your present or future wife. Pornography directs your desires to that of another person you do not know, will likely never meet, and who will remain in your view an object and item rather than a living, breathing human being made in God's image. Is that really the kind of life you want to have?

Another caution for men of any age is the role that lust plays in pornography. Now sexually desiring a woman is wonderful, but within certain God-ordained boundaries. That woman must be your wife and only your wife; as we talked about in the chapter on dating and marriage, God has wired our spiritual and emotional DNA for faithfulness. The goal of the entire pornographic industry (aside from the massive amounts of money it makes) is to get you to lust. Specifically, porn aims to have you lust in isolation from human relationship, and to act upon that lust, and to do so alone.

Another problem—one we've alluded to already—is that pornography ceases to excite the viewer unless he (1) increases his habit of porn viewership or (2) views images and activities of a 'harder-core' and more violent nature. This can lead to a greater chance of acting out the violence in physical or sexual damage on others. Lest you think this is assuming too much, consider that serial killer Ted Bundy—in his last interview before being executed—admitted that his addiction to pornography played heavily into his lifestyle of violence and evil. Then he said, *I've lived in prison for a long time now and I've met a lot of men who were motivated to commit violence just like me and without exception, every one of them was deeply involved in pornography.* This is not to say that if you view porn, then you will automatically become a death row serial murderer (though it doesn't improve your chances of avoidance). But it is true there is a noticeable link between pornography and violent crime.

A further threat for men is the neurological damage pornography does to the male brain. Consistent viewing of pornography rewires the brain's function and expectations for sexual pleasure and activity.[3] The chemical dopamine—which is produced as a pleasurable reward for doing things one enjoys—gets overproduced to the point where the dopamine cells begin to shrink and malfunction.[4] This, in essence, damages how the male senses and reacts to pleasurable things, and he begins to require more pornographic material and more shocking images to boost dopamine levels to usual amounts. All this is structural and wiring damage one inflicts on his bodily dwelling, appropriate language for the body given what the Apostle Paul states when he says, '[D]o you not know that your body is a temple of the Holy Spirit within you?' (1 Cor. 6:19).

If you're wondering if this is essentially like drug addiction, you'd be correct. But there's more. Pornography damages and shrinks the frontal lobe of the male brain as the dopamine cells suffer. This area acts as the restraint system on human action,

---

3. See https://salvomag.com/article/salvo13/slave-master

4. https://www.thegospelcoalition.org/article/9-things-you-should-know-about-pornography-and-the-brain/

and the damage done by porn means the person compromises his chances of discerning the consequences of his explosive addiction.[5] The ability of the male to critique the results of his decisions and to cultivate restraints on the nuclear capacity of his visual cavorting? It is severely hobbled at best and paralyzed at worst. As you can see, pornography is not a victimless activity. And the first victim is the viewer. If this is how porn works—with an eventual damage to your brain's secretions and abilities—then how can young men especially have such a cavalier attitude about it?

I would also offer a word for **women**, both young and older, on this matter. It is true that female viewership of pornography is less than the male percentages. Yet that doesn't mean it doesn't happen. And there are dangerous chances taken when a young female engages in sexting provocative pictures of herself via her iPhone or distributing them via her computer.

(1) First of all, once you send a picture of yourself out, you have lost control of where it goes next. Don't do this and pretend that you've made a wise choice or that you can trust the guys to whom you've sent the pictures. You can't.

(2) You have cheapened yourself. Guys already struggle with intimacy. Don't make it worse. Don't give other guys the impression that you are just a sexual object to be used and exploited.

(3) You are cheapening men. Females instead should push and encourage males to be honorable, dignified, and godly in their actions, words, and thoughts.

(4) You are severely wounding the odds for others—and just as critically, for yourself—to have genuine, authentic, and pure relationships in the future. Yes, humans sin.

---

5. https://www.lifestartherapy.com/what-your-brain-looks-like-on-pornography/

No doubt about that. But sexual sin strikes deeply at the core of your being. When you do give yourself to your husband for good, you don't want other fingerprints all over your soul.

'Now What?': Hitting Back With Grace and Holiness

Yes, dealing with sexual matters happens to be a difficult path. We live in a world that seems designed to puncture any chance one has of taking purity seriously. The availability of pornography at a few keystrokes of a computer or phone means that brutal temptation afflicts us around the clock. What chance does someone have if he or she really wants to forge a path pleasing to Christ?

First, consider how you are *positioning your life.* Where do you go and what are you doing in those places? What temptation is there? This can mean avoiding certain places in your community. It can also mean placing strategic barriers in your life. It's unreasonable to think you can stay away from your laptop or other personal digital devices. Your school assignments or your vocation depend significantly upon your functional capacity with a computer. But you can take willing steps to shield yourself by utilizing filters that will block access to pornographic sites. If you don't want temptation, think about what you watch on cable or satellite or streaming television, or even if you need such luxuries.

Next, think about how open you are to *accountability.* Are there people in your life with whom you can be real and authentic? Can they ask you the probing questions and challenge you? Can they encourage you with God's grace even as they hold you to God's holiness? I know this can be an incredibly difficult step, especially for guys. It takes commitment to transparency and the willingness to be known, warts and all, by others. I would ask if this is important enough to you. Peter reminded his readers that giving in to temptation is not an option when he told them

> *Set your hope fully on the grace that will be brought to you at the revelation of Jesus Christ. As obedient children, do not be conformed to the passions of your former ignorance, but as he who called you is holy, you also be holy in all your conduct, since it is written, 'You shall be holy, for I am holy'* (1 Pet. 1:13b-16).

Whom do you trust with the harshest, darkest corners of your soul? Don't say, 'Well, I can get by on my own strength.' Anyone who deliberately removes themselves from accountability, no matter how sincere they are, is headed for a fall.

Finally, beyond human connection and help, you need to know that succeeding against pornographic temptation and activity is **impossible** unless Jesus is in the midst of your struggles. When Christ told His disciples that *apart from Him, they could do nothing* (John 15:5), it applies to us today. Sin is more powerful than you and I can imagine, but by turning yourself over in prayer and asking for the help of the Holy Spirit, there is abundant hope to meet those challenges and snares. God's help is always there, and exhibiting faith by taking Him at His word and acting upon it is the center point of battling all temptation.

For Your Consideration

- What do you think is the major challenge pornography poses today? Is it the accessibility of it on the Internet? The intense level of addiction to it? The neurological damage it poses? The devastating results it can bring? Justify your answer.

- Why is pornography something both single and married people should resist?

- How might you be held accountable by someone if you struggle with pornography?

15

Homosexuality and Same-Sex Marriage

ONCE when our family was visiting my Uncle Red's clan in western Pennsylvania, we kids took a walk out in the fields surrounding their rural home. Upon hearing a distant alert from Aunt Joan that dinner was on the table, we ran toward the house, and I—wanting to take a shortcut—attempted a quick and unwieldy side-hurdle over an electric wire fence for which I thought I had clearance. My right foot stuck in the soft earth and I couldn't lift it over in time before receiving a thump to my body that lifted me a few inches off the ground. My younger brother, upon listening to my later tale of woe, replied, 'What did you expect getting so close to that thing?'

I wonder if some people—Christian or not—might have the same inclination regarding a discussion on homosexuality and same-sex marriage. This matter has all the potential to breed civil conversation as successfully as a spark breeds safety in a gunpowder factory. *What do we expect getting so close to this issue?* This is especially the case as society displays greater open-ness to a range of sexual attitudes and behaviors. *Are well-meaning, faithful Christians just asking for trouble wading into this thing? And is homosexuality such a big deal?*

Just for the record, we're diving in.

'What?': The Homosexual Condition

It's important to distinguish between homosexual (or same-sex) *attraction and inclination* and homosexual *activity and behavior*. Same-sex <u>attraction</u> means that one is overwhelmingly physically and/or sexually attracted to members of the same gender as they are (I use sex and gender to mean the same thing here; more on that in a later chapter). It remains a mystery where these desires originate. We can have theories, but in all truth, we don't know. The Bible *never* specifically addresses what causes same-sex attraction; it speaks to homosexual activity and behavior. And in my conversations with former students and acquaintances who struggle with same-sex attraction, it seems clear they have no idea how these attractions arise.

One student of mine from years ago cried as he told me he was sexually attracted to other males. He desperately wanted *not* to be homosexual. Even as he refused to act upon his impulses, he shared with me that his feelings baffled him beyond description. Another young man—speaking at an assembly at my school—was asked if he believed people 'choose to be gay.' Shaking his head vigorously from side to side, he declared, 'Absolutely not. Who would willingly sign up for that?' He made a good point. With whatever stigma and health issues that would come with the homosexual lifestyle, one wonders why someone would select feelings that could lead toward that end.

However, in distinguishing between same-sex attraction and same-sex activity, some might believe this means the attraction is neutral or good while the activity is wrong. Some Christians even try to make this case. The problem is that there is nothing in the Bible nor in the overwhelmingly majority of Christian tradition that supports this. If we have an attraction or desire to commit an activity that is not noble, good, or life-giving, it is critical for followers of Jesus to seek to work against it and, in Paul's words in Colossians, put both those desires and behaviors to death. Think about it this way: Would it be fine for a husband to have adulterous sexual desires for women other than his wife, so long as he doesn't participate in adulterous relationships?[1] Is it okay to have feelings of rage as long as you don't murder someone? Is overwhelming greed permissible so long as one doesn't steal or shoplift? Is a person who has pedophiliac passions in the clear as long as he doesn't act out on his impulses? It seems clear that—both biblically and in common sense logic—the answers to those questions would be no.

Same-sex activity and behavior is another matter to consider. First of all, there are plenty of places in Scripture that address this expression of sexuality. Secondly, even if one rejects Biblical authority, human construction and the consequences of homosexual activity both speak against this lifestyle.

Same-sex behavior takes a wide range of expression (which doesn't require exhaustive detail in a book of this length). Yet whether or not the sexual dalliances are casual hookups or moments woven into the fabric of a committed same-sex partnership, the ultimate physical apex of such behavior is eroticized, genital sexual activity. Yes, we have already defined that before with heterosexual behavior and emphasized that we are wired for sexual activity within heterosexual, monogamous marriage. Is there any room for that for homosexuals?

'So What?': The Bible Speaks

The Bible addresses homosexual behavior and activity in two ways: through *declarative* and *narrative passages*. In both testaments, we find declarative passages of principles or

---

1. Ladies, would *you* be happy with a man for whom this was the case?

commands. In Leviticus 18:22, God speaks to Moses that *'You shall not lie with a man as with a woman; it is an abomination.'* Two chapters later, we run across a catalog of punishments for sexual immorality. Tucked away in that list, we find these words: *'If a man lies with a male as with a woman, both of them have committed an abomination; they shall surely be put to death; their blood is upon them'* (Lev. 20:13). Even though the civil/criminal aspects of the Law of Moses are no longer specifically binding in the New Covenant era, the fact that erotic homosexual activity merited this punishment shows the seriousness with which God views it.

The declarative passages continue in the New Testament. The Apostle Paul notes the actions of certain rebellious humans in Romans 1, who are so deep into their sinful revelry that *'God gave them up to dishonorable passions. For their women exchanged natural relations for those that are contrary to nature; and the men likewise gave up natural relations with women and were consumed with passion for one another, men committing shameless acts with men and receiving in themselves the due penalty for their error'* (vv. 26-27). Writing his first letter to the energetic yet immorality-stained church at Corinth, Paul places *'those who practice homosexuality'* under the umbrella of consistent, unrepentant members of those who 'will not inherit the kingdom of God' (1 Cor. 6:9).

Even in the narrative, historical passages of Scripture, homosexual behavior is cast in a most disapproving light. In Genesis 19:4-5, the male population of the city of Sodom (from which we get the term *sodomy*) lays siege to the house of Lot, who is providing dinner and shelter for two travelers (spoiler alert: they're angels). The citizens' demand is rather chilling when they call out, *'Where are the men who came to you tonight? Bring them out that we may know* (i.e., have sex with) *them?'* Lot begs them not to act so wickedly and barely escapes with his life, a story you can read for yourself in Genesis 19. For that sinful streak, and a host of others (listed in Ezek. 16:49-50), Sodom was vaporized the next morning with a fire-and-brimstone attack from God's hand.[2]

In Judges 19, we find a repeat of this demand in Gibeah during Israel's time of waywardness after they possessed their promised land of Canaan. A citizen of Gibeah provides dinner and shelter for a priest and his companion when the 'worthless fellows' of the city surround the house and insist they be given the priest for a savage sex romp. The master of the house refused, but a series of incidents following from this standoff still led to civil war.

Think about the words that become the taglines when the Bible specifically addresses homosexual activity: *abomination, dishonorable, contrary to nature, not inherit the kingdom of God, wickedly, worthless.* There should be no doubt these descriptions are abundantly clear about how what God has not created humanity for. A number of people will attempt to shift words and claim homosexuality is not the area of criticism in these passages, but the text and intent of Scripture don't allow for that kind of wiggle room.

There are objections to these Biblical directives from some who will claim, 'Wait! *Jesus* never said anything about gay

---

2. Some will argue that the sin of Sodom has nothing to do with homosexuality and its exhibition, but rather because of the lack of hospitality of the citizens to Lot's visitors, which they were trying to rectify by saying they wanted to 'know' the angelic guests (Gen. 19:5). This re-interpretation of the passage falls apart, though, when given Lot's initial actions and his response to the townsmen. First, he strongly urges the visitors to not spend the night in the city square, likely because they'd be sexually assaulted. And he doesn't remind the Sodomites they were being rude; he says 'Do not act so *wickedly*' (Gen. 19:7). These details lead us to the conclusion that homosexuality (and the homosexual gang rape they desired) was one of the reasons for Sodom's destruction. For a concise exposition and application of this passage, see Dale Ralph Davis' *Faith of Our Father: Expositions of Genesis 12–25* (Fearn, Ross-shire, UK: Christian Focus Publications, 2015), pp. 106-110.

marriage!' And that is true in a way. The Bible never *records* Jesus as having said anything specific about homosexual behavior during His earthly ministry. That silence, however, is not enough to claim that Jesus would say it was a legitimate or healthy activity. Jesus, as a Jew, would have accepted the entire Scriptures (at that time the Old Testament) as the authoritative Word of God. When He quoted from Scripture and appealed to its authority, He would say *'You have heard it said ...'* During more than one of His appeals to Scripture, Jesus confirmed that marriage was to be solely between one man and one woman (Mark 10:6-9). Plus, as a Jew by upbringing, Jesus would have accepted the Old Testament prohibitions against homosexual behavior, so why would there be a pressing need for Him to comment further? And consider the other things that weren't part of Jesus' commentary. He never spoke against incestuous sexual relationships between close family members. He never is recorded as having said anything specific about rape. (Or poisoning someone's sandwich. Or poor road maintenance. Well, you get the point.) Does His lack of speech on an issue mean He believes it is okay to commit a specific act? It would appear the answer is no.

'So What?': Other Considerations

Aside from the Biblical statements about homosexual behavior, what else makes the homosexual lifestyle a critical issue today?

Public health concerns can intersect with homosexual practice. The obvious subject here is the persistence of the Human Immunodeficiency Virus (HIV) which can develop into Acquired Immune Deficiency Syndrome (AIDS). The best studies from the Centers for Disease Control estimate that 1.2 million people in the United States are presently living with HIV, with a steady level of fifty thousand people becoming newly infected each year. While a considerable number of new HIV infections in America are the result of heterosexual intercourse, sharing of dirty needles in intravenous drug usage, and tainted blood transfusions, the majority (roughly six out of every ten) of new HIV infections are found in homosexual and bisexual men. Metropolitan areas in the American South (such as Miami, Orlando, Atlanta, New Orleans, and Jackson, MS) with high minority populations have been hit particularly hard. In addition, homosexual and bisexual men display a much higher rate of contracting other viral diseases like hepatitis A, B, and C.[3]

Another concerning phenomenon can be the relative impermanence of homosexual relationships. There are many exceptions to this rule, for a number of gays and lesbians might remain in committed same-sex relationships for extensive periods of time. Studies of HIV-positive men have revealed a high level of promiscuity in these tribes, with an average number of partners in the hundreds. With this seeming tendency to move from liaison to liaison, there seems to be very little evidence for chaste commitment in large swathes of the homosexual community. [To be fair, there can be many heterosexuals who demonstrate the same recklessness in their libido.]

Yet another area of attention is the ongoing conversation about same-sex marriage. On June 26, 2015, the United States Supreme Court—in the case of *Obergefell v. Hodges*—ruled by a 5-4 decision that people of the same sex could now get legally married anywhere in the United States, as it struck down any state bans on what was commonly called 'gay marriage' or 'marriage equality.' While this action brought happiness to many and shock to others, it was a point toward which America had been moving for some time. In 2004, 60 per cent of Americans *opposed* same-sex marriage, compared

---

3. https://www.cdc.gov/hiv/pdf/statistics/overview/cdc-hiv-us-ataglance.pdf

to 31 per cent who *supported* it. Now the numbers essentially reversed themselves, with Americans who support same-sex marriage outranking those who oppose it by 61 to 31 per cent.[4] Clearly, the marriage equality movement has picked up a lot of momentum. Just as clearly, those who believe that marriage should be reserved for one man with one woman need to think wisely about how to craft their own ideas and engage with those who disagree.[5]

'Now What?': A Persuasive Case for Biblical Sexuality

We have previously crafted a layered argument for sexual activity taking place in a faithful, committed marriage between one husband and one wife. But why can't people of the same gender have their own relationships and get married? Isn't the fact they love each other enough? Those are questions that deserve gracious and solid answers.

First, while it's true that everyone who gets married will enter a new existence of particular challenges and complications (we are talking about a sinner marrying a fellow sinner, after all), we've already seen that the homosexual lifestyle tends to be more fraught with health and relational instability than its heterosexual counterpart. While this does not automatically disqualify homosexual relationships on that point alone, it is a serious reality to consider.

Another question to press is, 'Why would love be the central issue?' While love is an essential ingredient for a dating or marriage relationship to flourish and grow, we can think of

---

4. https://www.pewforum.org/fact-sheet/changing-attitudes-on-gay-marriage/

5. Interestingly enough, the data shows that acceptance of lesbian, gay, bisexual, transgender, and queer people has dropped for two straight years among adults between 18 and 34 years of age. See https://www.newsweek.com/young-people-comfortable-lgbt-poll-1445435

other taboo romances such as where people may 'fall in love' or have (to them) meaningful levels of affection. The incestuous rendezvous, the adulterous tryst, or an affair between boss and subordinate at work might be marked by sensations and declarations of love, but these stirrings—however construed—do not mean the entanglement is wholesome, noble, or honorable. So, while love must be in the mix, there must be more to this. If it comes down to love and consent, then logically this would open the door to allowing unions like polygamy (many spouses) and others.[6]

While we have looked at what Scripture says about homosexual behavior (which we would logically assume would take place within same-sex marriage), we have to realize that not everyone will accept the authority of the Bible. Thus, it raises the question: Can one make an argument against homosexual activity even when you take God out of the equation? We can try in the following fashion:

(1) For the sake of argument, if we have a world without God, we are left with a planet of competing species, of which it seems humankind is the dominant species that forges culture and meaningful existence.

(2) If humankind exists, it seems logical that for it to flourish, humanity must continue to survive and exist. The way to survive is to keep the human species reproducing.

(3) For the human species to reproduce, there must be a union of gametes (sperm and egg) from a male and a female. It cannot be a shared union of male to male gametes or female

---

6. This is not to say that same-sex marriage will quickly usher in legitimacy of polygamy, polyamory, incest, and other sexual relationships. I simply mean that reducing sexual action to love and consent means that there is no logical barrier to these other matters. One doesn't have a leg to stand on if they say, 'Yes, I'm for gay marriage, but I don't believe incest and polygamy are legitimate.'

to female gametes. Human survival demands reproduction that requires a heterosexual union of some kind.

(4) From this, we see that heterosexual union at the cellular level provides a furtherance of the human race that same-sex union can never provide. Because of this generational advancement, we can conclude that hetero-sexual connection fulfills the nature of humanity in a way that same-sex connection cannot.

(5) From this, we can conclude that—in a secular worldview where one ignores the being of God and the reality of divine revelation—even if one doesn't think in terms of 'sinfulness', one can conclude that homosexual behavior is—at its core—inferior to heterosexual behavior and falls short of affirming the full depth of human dignity, survival, and existence. And because this behavior is truly inferior in any attempt to create flourishing in the human race, it is *subhuman* activity.

(6) Given that marriage is an institution in which the reality of (1) through (5) above take place, same-sex marriage ends up being inferior to heterosexual marriage and does not affirm human-ness in a way that enables it to flourish.

'Now What?': Affirming Truth While Reaching Out

While the Bible makes clear statements that condemn homo-sexual behavior, and while one can make a secular argument toward similar conclusions, Christians must never resign them-selves merely to throwing grenades of condemnation toward people who engage in homosexual activity or struggle with same-sex attraction. Thankfully, it seems to me that more serious Christians are wanting to move beyond condemnation toward compassionate conversation, into an area where one can hold to Biblical convictions but also participate in civil engagement. In other words, one can disagree with someone's views and sexual mores without being disagreeable. But some who desire this might not know where to begin. I offer the following suggestions:

(1) A key aspect of friendship that people—homosexuals included—are looking for is winsomeness. Even if you disagree with the lifestyle and sexual choices of an individual, can you articulate your beliefs in a decent, humane manner that demonstrates compassion for them while rooted in your own convictions?

(2) Homosexuals—and really, all people—want Christians to be authentic, to admit their own failings and shortcomings and need for forgiveness in their own brokenness. Being open about one's own struggles and the need to corral personal lusts is a powerful connection. That spirit can create a genuine community that makes people of differing backgrounds more comfortable with others and issues of faith.

(3) Consistently differentiate between same-sex attraction and same-sex behavior. You might find that a significant number of people struggle with same-sex attraction but—whether out of fear over compromising their health or their desire to live a chaste life or for whatever reason—actively resist engaging in homosexual activity. Remember that while we must always battle against lustful temptation or attraction of any stripe, we should quickly encourage those who avoid and turn away from acting on their impulses.

(4) Be able to speak firmly yet graciously when asked if homosexuals can be Christian believers or have a

'relationship with God'. First of all, what does that phrase mean? If one means having a strong sense of wanting to be 'religious', that's an attempt anyone can make. But if we're talking about being a follower of Jesus Christ, we have to remember that part of walking in grace means willfully submitting to the holiness that God requires. This means working through homosexual temptation and saying no to homosexual activity, and to repent of one's failings. To be completely fair, it also means fighting against lustful heterosexual temptation and refusing to satisfy one's urges outside of faithful, monogamous marriage. It means saying no to greed, theft, dishonesty, and a host of other sins. Everyone has to ask, 'If I am to follow Christ, then what is Christ asking of me?' And if your desires and actions are consistently and willfully off track from what Jesus says, you have to seriously question your commitment to Him.

(5) Make a commitment to be an increasingly empathetic individual. Think about what it is like to be in another person's shoes, another fellow human being's skin. Remember that if you're a Christian, you follow a Savior who literally **took on human flesh!** Unless we know each other's life stories, we don't really know the occurrences that lead us to sexual broken-ness. Yes, people are responsible for their actions, but they also have personal histories and events that influence their choices. There can be a whole host of reasons for the way someone functions, and we at least need to be willing to understand that even if we reject how they choose to behave.

(6) Correct any misconceptions you may have about homo-sexuals. One glaring error people—especially Christians

—can make is to assume homosexuals have nothing to teach us about life or contribute to our existence and enjoyment. What we find instead is that God's creative gifts and astounding capabilities have been given to all people in some measure thanks to His common grace. Some of the greatest life lessons are found in literature written by homosexuals. A number of my favorite actors are gay. Homosexual individuals are amongst the movers and shakers in the business world and marketplace, bringing cutting-edge goods and services to our fingertips. And you can be friends with someone who is gay or lesbian even if you don't agree with their actions. God can and will bless you through the efforts of others who are radically different than you. Are they sinners? Yes. Am I? Definitely. Are you? Of course! Whom else does God have to work with?

For Your Consideration

- Many different terms get thrown around … same-sex attraction, same-sex orientation, same-sex activity/behavior. Has this chapter changed how you view those ideas? Would you define any of these ideas differently than the author, and why?

- The author names several categories in building a case that homosexuality is sinful and harmful. Out of the categories named (Biblical statements, public health concerns, impermanence of relationships), which do you find the most compelling one?

- Why is love and consent not a good enough reason to legitimize a particular romantic arrangement? Is the secular argument (reasons numbered 1-6 in 'A Persuasive Case for Biblical Sexuality') a strong one to demonstrate the shortcomings of homosexual behavior?

- What are some ways you can be gracious and empathetic toward homosexuals even if you disagree with their lifestyle? What if someone says 'I was born this way' or 'Love me – love my lifestyle'?

16

Transgenderism and Gender Identities

WHEN I was a youngster (think five or six years old), we lived in a small house in Louisville, Kentucky, where my father was laboring through his doctoral dissertation. In those days before flat-screen televisions, we had a small, fifteen-inch TV set that sat in the living room. Connected to it was an antenna, and if we wanted to change channels, we had to get up from where we sat, walk to the TV, and turn the buttons on it if we wanted to switch from NBC to CBS or ABC or PBS. I didn't mind changing the channels by hand. The one thing I did have an issue with, even in my tender years, was having access to only a handful of channels. The ones I listed above were pretty much it, as we lived before cable and satellite television. It was your situation, take it or leave it, and if the President of the United States was making a televised address, every station carried it and your regular programs or cartoons or whatever you wanted to watch got pre-empted. But the era was a simpler one. You knew what you could expect from television. Now we live in an age of over-selection. There seem to be as many television channels as there are stars in the sky. There's a plethora of choices in *who* provides those channels (your local cable company? SlingTV?

DirecTV? YouTubeTV? Others?). Previously, we aligned ourselves with what was available; now the ground has shifted.

The ground has shifted in the world of what is commonly called gender identity. When I was in fourth grade taking school achievement tests, you had to mark the paper answer sheet with some rudimentary facts about yourself. In the box marked 'sex', you could fill in the bubble next to either 'male' or 'female'. That was it; the world was gender binary. Two genders, male and female, existed, and every human person was one of those two. Now we hear of a cornucopia of identities and labels: transgender, pangender, gender fluid, omnisexual, and others. There are various reasons for this cultural shift, but we'll encounter these after providing some definitions and clarifying the assumptions of gender identity.

'What?': The Shape of the Movement

It would take longer paper and time than I presently have to comprehensively present coverage of these matters, so we will not go into much technical depth. But a few things can be made clear. We have seen a considerable rise in the visibility and voice of individuals who consider themselves as *transgender*. Even defining transgender can take us in a couple directions. A baseline definition of transgender would be people who do not identify with their birth sex. A person who was born a male might experience or interpret various sensations while growing up, sensations that might lead the person to believe he is more 'female' instead. A further extension of this definition occurs when the person in question identifies so strongly with the opposite gender that he desires to alter his appearance and sex characteristics (through hormone therapy and/or sex reassignment surgery).[1] Another category is *gender fluidity*. This means

---

1. https://eca.state.gov/files/bureau/sogi_terminology.pdf

that an individual's internal sense of being male, female, a mixture of both sexes, or neither of them, might be in constant flux. The feelings of discomfort or anxiety one senses that come from whatever lack of 'matching up' with one's anatomy is sometimes defined as *gender dysphoria.*[2] One more category for our purposes is that of people who qualify as *intersex*, that is, they are born with reproductive anatomy that doesn't match their male or female biology. For example, a girl might (unbeknownst to her) have testicles that develop unnoticed until much later in life. We will return to the matter of intersex persons later in the 'Now What' section as this is largely a separate issue for practical application.

Aside from these categories, perhaps you are noticing a trend amongst those who identify as transgender and gender fluid. That is, there is the assertion that *what one feels about the self can differ from one's own anatomy.* The vision that a man or woman, a boy or girl, has about their identity is a matter which is independent from one's sexual biology. In short, any integrated connection between identity and biology—or to put it another way, between self-awareness and the body—is not necessarily there. This is not a perspective that is going away, and many governments have pressed for protection of transgendered and gender fluid persons, in particular. Legislation on these matters ranges from states in the U.S. letting transgender individuals use public restrooms that match the gender with which they identify[3] to levying fines up to a quarter-million dollars against people who refer to trans-sexuals by the natural gender.[4] Cross-gender

---

2. https://www.apa.org/pi/lgbt/resources/sexuality-definitions.pdf

3. https://ballotpedia.org/Transgender_bathroom_access_laws_in_the_United_States. Eighteen states, plus the District of Columbia, have such laws.

4. https://www.lifesitenews.com/news/nyc-will-fine-employers-up-to-250000-for-referring-to-transsexuals-by-their. People are expected to refer to others by their 'preferred pronoun'.

feelings and sensations, if one has them, are experiences to be embraced as healthy and liberating advances toward the true self, we are told. Transgendered individuals are now recognized and celebrated for their actions, boldness, and achievements. Caitlyn Jenner, formerly known as the male Olympian gold medal-winning decathlete Bruce Jenner, received the Arthur Ashe Courage Award in a notable media tribute at the 2015 ESPY Awards.[5]

'So What?': The Problems with the Movement

One foundational issue with this gender identity question is the separation of body and identity. What one desires to do becomes so riven from one's physical nature that people begin to believe that what counts is their sense of themselves, no matter what their body demonstrates. In the gender identity movement, sex organs become arbitrary. What matters is what one *feels* about their own person. This creates a dangerous divorce between the physical world and our psychological sense that has already shown up in other areas.

In abortion, people might divorce the idea of the unborn child's body from the sense of any right to live as a person. In extramarital sex—whether the heterosexual or homosexual variety—people excuse their action by divorcing their desires from any sense of bodily function. It's not whether or not things are healthy for us or strengthen our bodies, but whether we want to indulge in them because we have these desires.[6]

If we are mere animals with rugged passions and there's no point to life other than just doing what we want, there's no

---

5. https://espnpressroom.com/us/press-releases/2015/06/caitlyn-jenner-to-be-honored-with-the-arthur-ashe-courage-award-at-the-2015-espys-on-abc-july-15/

6. Nancy Pearcey does an incredible job exposing the holes in this worldview in her *Love Thy Body: Answering Hard Questions about Life and Sexuality* (Grand Rapids, MI: Baker Books, 2018).

problem with this. But if we are made for a purpose by a God for His purposes and we are constructed in a unity of body and identity, then any attempt to split this unity will be disastrous. You will not nourish your body but rather destroy your very self.

Aside from the philosophical divorce between body and identity that ignores the body as a good creation of God, this perspective is non-sensical if we substitute other matters. Perhaps you say there is no problem if I want to identify as a female. Fair enough. You can say that. Can I participate in female sports and win awards and championships there? That madness is already occurring, as biologically male students are destroying competitions and records and making a mockery of female high school athletics.[7] But the theatre of the ludicrous doesn't end there. Suppose I want to identify as wealthy? Certainly I could say that. The only problem (or the chief one of many, not to mention my sanity) would be my bank account doesn't match how I identify myself. Wouldn't you think some level of financial assets would reinforce the claim to wealth? Wouldn't I need assets, cash, stock portfolio, and other credits to my name to make my claim mean anything? What if I want to be referred to as 'Dr Davis'? Doesn't the lack of a medical degree or the academic achievement of a PhD diploma make that claim laughable, no matter how sincerely I seem to believe my own assertion?[8] Can I claim British, Finnish, German, or Italian citizenship if I've never taken any legal steps to secure those 'identities' beyond mental sensation or verbal entreaty?

---

7. https://nypost.com/2019/03/04/trans-athletes-are-making-a-travesty-of-womens-sports/

8. It strikes me that if we are going to point out the holes in gender identity theory and transgenderism, then we really need to speak out against those who embellish their resumes and achievements with titles and positions they've never earned. These are distinct issues, but gender fluidity and transgenderism isn't always motivated by deceit like padding one's professional description is.

Can I identify as cheese (yes, *cheese*) even though I am neither Swiss, Munster, brie, nor cheddar? I know that last statement is the most ridiculous of all the above, but I'm concerned for the principle. If you make a claim of identity, what is there to back it up beyond your 'inner sense' (which can radically change on a whim, by the way)?

Defining sexual identity on the basis of self-feeling is really the latest expression of an issue the human race has brought upon itself for some time. We have to ask the question, 'How do we know what we know?' If our appraisal of our gender, of our very nature, is our call, how do we know we are making the proper judgment? Is truth a matter of what we feel, or is truth something that is established outside of ourselves? Calling ourselves whatever we desire has its limits.

This reminds me of a story about Abraham Lincoln, President of the United States during what is often called the American Civil War. Lincoln was hosting a gathering of Northern military personnel and generals regarding what the Union's strategy should be against the Confederacy while fighting on Southern soil. The military men offered a litany of possibilities, framed constantly with the words, 'Suppose (this)' or 'Suppose (that)'. Finally, Lincoln had enough of their hedging and said, 'Well, suppose you call a sheep's tail a leg. How many legs would it have?' One general said, 'It'd have five,' to which Lincoln retorted, 'No, no! Calling a sheep's tail a leg doesn't make it a leg! It would still only have four legs! The tail is still a tail!'[9] There's a real danger in assigning reality to whatever we might want it to be rather than what it is.

Ultimately, the line is drawn between two possibilities: Either we are human beings who are fashioned as either male or female from the start, or our conception of ourselves is up for

---

9. My father used this story in a sermon once. I have no clue what the source is.

grabs with the self as the prime definer. Scripture lays out the construction of the human species from the beginning as two sexes, created and defined by a Creator God, and thus gender aligns with sexual construction.

'So God created man in his own image, in the image of God he created him: male and female he created them' (Gen. 1:27). Notice that the sexual beings, Adam and Eve, are male and female and both reflect God's image, as a finite yet treasured imprint of God's residue, so to speak. To push back against the male-female dichotomy and reality is to sully the image of God in humanity. And when we smudge this, there are devastating results. If we can make or define ourselves, who needs a Creator? And if we don't need a Creator, who needs the order that comes from creation? We become creatures who desire our own manufactured chaos (as long as it is of our own doing) rather than submit to orderly direction.

Even if you or others don't accept the Bible as authoritative, we are still left with clearly defined genders versus chaos defined by the individual based on what he or she 'feels to be'. Aside from the social chaos that can erupt from this, the rampant self-definition of transgenderism (by self-image, hormones, or surgery) and gender fluidity confuses and waters down the idea of legal rights. In an age where one can be what they define themselves to be, how do we know what protections they deserve?

'Now What?': Engaging the Movement

What I've written above might seem hard-hitting; it's actually just born from a desire to make the lines abundantly clear. We should not leave our engagement solely to that territory. These are not policy arguments, but a chance to come alongside others who might experience a discrepancy between their bodies and their understandings, or people whose family members are conflicted along these lines. And the spirit in which we do so is one of compassion.[10]

Everyone has a different story. As such, the words 'transgender' or 'gender fluid' can be loaded with personal weight. For some people, the issue is one of real biology. Nearly four million babies in the United States, for example, are born every year. Of that number, nearly one thousand are born intersex, with some irregularities in the development of sexual organs as we've described previously.[11] Others have a psychological sense of being 'trapped' in the wrong body. Still others might have had gender reassignment surgery and already regret the results. Thus, when you encounter others for whom the gender identity map is very convoluted, get to know them and hear out their story. That gives you a place at their table if they ask questions.

Another reason for compassion is that transgender and gender fluid people deal with the weight of their perceived identity. Transgender adolescents are at least twice as likely to attempt suicide than other teens who are not transgender.[12] You can always put together a list of reasons you think why this is the case, but the truth is there is a lot of pain in this community. That deserves empathy, one would think.

A foundational approach to encountering transgender and gender fluid people is having a firm, biblical understanding of

---

10. A good chunk of what follows comes from Dr Dan Doriani, my former New Testament professor, in his post at https://www.placefortruth.org/blog/the-transgender-moment-and-the-technological-imperative

11. Granted, that's only 0.025% of the live births each year, too low to be, as Doriani says, 'the root of the transgender wave'. In fairness, though, that's more than the number of boys born each year with X-linked myotubular myopathy, which afflicts our son. If I hope for the best for Joshua and other boys like him, I should be able to extend compassion to the category of intersex individuals whose population is even higher.

12. https://www.reuters.com/article/us-health-transgender-teen-suicide/trans-teens-much-more-likely-to-attempt-suicide

the goodness of the human body. In an age where advertising and visual media push the ideal weight, height, and appearance of one's body in our faces 24/7, we need to resist any urging to have our bodies 'measure up' to some mythical standard. We are created for glory and distinction, and our physical construction is a good thing. This will not remove some people's sense of confusion or frustration over their bodies and identity but exhibiting a humble confidence in who God has made us to be can be an attractive starting point that can inspire others.

We also need to recapture a healthy biblical understanding about the bringing about of human life. Oliver O'Donovan points out that, in the Bible, reproduction is described in a precise manner. Parents *beget* children; they do not *make* them. We bring forth beings like ourselves, who grow toward adulthood. Transgender re-assignment surgery is a technical manner of *making* life, or a new humanity, that conflicts with an understanding of humanity that begets.[13] And we must be especially wary of the results on the other side of techniques such as re-assignment surgery for 'gender transition.' Ryan T. Anderson notes in his book *When Harry Became Sally* that even technically successful surgeries don't address the psycho-social issues that remain. The most thorough tracking of post-surgical transgender persons demonstrates that their suicide rate is twenty times that of others.[14] Other factors show there is no evidence that gender re-assignment surgery results in a more healthy, fulfilling life for its recipients. That doesn't sound like a life of wholeness or happiness, and bullying can't fully account for that spike in rates. It sounds like people are taking on a lifestyle that doesn't mesh with the

---

13. This is from O'Donovan's *Begotten, Not Made*, referred to in Doriani's post.

14. https://www.heritage.org/gender/commentary/sex-reassignment-doesnt-work-here-the-evidence

emotional-spiritual-physical DNA we have as humans. And that should provoke compassion from others, not a spirit of 'I told you that it doesn't match the social narrative!'

Compassion, at its heart, is not about hearing people out and kindly letting them do whatever they desire to do. If an alcoholic friend wants to attempt drinking a keg of beer, preventing him from doing so is a measure of true compassion, not cruelty! Listening to others is a key part of this, but so is getting them to see that actions have consequences. We have a chance to help others to notice that this is not something that is just a matter of preference or personal taste or inner identity, but that there are choices and desires that are healthy and make for a stronger, better life. And transgender transitioning or activity is not a matter of mere preference.

Granted, there are some things in life that are issues of personal choice or taste. If I like peanut butter and Mackinac Fudge swirl ice cream and you like salted caramel ice cream better, those are matters of taste (literally and figuratively). But what if you are about to purchase a vehicle, and you have the option of either a 1990 Plymouth Sundance or a 2016 Toyota Sienna?[15] The Sundance's chassis emits a grinding noise, needs a new quart of oil every thousand miles, and the brake fluid chamber clogs up. The Sienna purrs along, handles well, and its safety features are immaculate. If you say, 'Well, I just happen to like the Sundance better. I'll get that!' If I am truly compassionate, am I going to let you purchase and drive around a potential death trap that will suck your bank account

---

15. Advance apologies to any and all Plymouth Sundance owners (if there are any of these cars still running). I merely desire to use them in a hypothetical analogy! And full disclosure: I own a Toyota Sienna, so there's some bias here. This car argument has been used by other Christian thinkers in other areas. I first encountered it in a different form in John Burke's *No Perfect People Allowed* (Grand Rapids, MI: Zondervan, 2007).

dry? No, the truly compassionate approach would be to nudge you toward the Sienna, the more beneficial car, the one that will safely and efficiently transport you and your family with fewer headaches (and hospital bills). If we know that results of the transgender lifestyle and transitioning are fraught with difficulty, we need to be agents of true compassion and firmly yet graciously warn people about them. Counseling and therapy are more fitting options that don't bring the irreversible nature of surgery.

Maybe that's not a conversation you envision having. But there is low-hanging fruit you can reach to engage this issue. For one, you can pray. Pray that if God brings people into your life that struggle with gender identity, you will be someone who shines a compassionate light into their dark struggles. Given the severe physical and mental health risks that come from gender transitioning, pray that the problems inherent with these paths will come to light and prevent others from seeking such a radical and inhumane approach to their struggles.

There is another action we can take. There can still be much cultural pressure toward gender stereotypes that can be unhealthy, and we must watch out for this. Boys can feel pressured to gravitate toward contact sports, hunting, and the like, while boys who discover giftedness in watercolor painting or culinary arts can be marginalized. Likewise, girls who seem less feminine can receive a fair bit of scoffing. Seriously, is there any rule that a girl can't change the oil or air filters in an automobile or do bed-frame carpentry? Pigeonholing males or females into areas that conflict with the gifts God gives them does great harm to their growing awareness of who they are created to be, and it implies that God did a lousy job making them. Instead, can we have confidence in Scripture to display what it means to be created in God's image, whether we are male or female? If we can begin there, then we are on the right track.

For Your Consideration

- Why do you think we are seeing more people 'identifying' as a different gender or no gender at all? In other words, why do we have this increase in self-determination this way?

- What other problems might you see arising from asserting different sexual or gender identities?

- How could you demonstrate compassion and understanding toward someone who is genuinely born intersex, for example?

PART FOUR
STEWARDSHIP MATTERS

WE have seen that our view on human life is essential, and our understanding of human relationships makes a profound impact upon the way we live. Now we enter a connected series of issues, and they continue along a logical progression. Within life, we engage in relationships, and within these relationships we need to steward (take care of) things in our individual possessions, our workplaces, our natural environments, and the world's increasingly mobile people groups.

Stewardship is intentional. No one backs into a mastery of it. Taking care of what is entrusted to us takes discipline and care. Sometimes we will find it difficult to be faithful, but God demands it of us. And even though we might discern general direction from the Bible and common sense, sometimes our location and specific situations might mean we apply stewardship in different ways. For example, a family with an income of seventy thousand dollars per year will make particular decisions about housing and spending that differ from a family making two hundred thousand dollars. Laws on immigration may differ between, say, the United States and Great Britain, so a legal officer in Oklahoma might have a dissimilar response to a social worker in Portsmouth. Environmental principles vary depending where one lives, so ranchers in Nebraska and Kansas may have distinct responses to matters than a dairy farmer near Inverness.

But in spite of being unique people in a myriad of circumstances, how we steward what God sends our way is supremely important. Details now follow.

17

Personal Stewardship

WHEN our son was working through his high school years, we had considerable freedom to determine what would work best for his learning. Such is the advantage of homeschooling. As he entered his final year of high school, we wanted him to have one more year of mathematics, but he wasn't the type to mash his way through theoretical courses of algebra or geometry, let alone calculus. Our solution was that he should take consumer math (sometimes called business math). Over the course of the school year, Joshua worked out practical matters like purchasing the best possible life insurance policy, how to select the best deal on a deep freezer, computing interest on a loan, and preparing an income tax return. One unit involved setting a personal budget for a month and prioritizing what percentage of income he would spend on food, transportation, utilities, leisure, and so forth. Crunching these numbers took some time, and the necessary diligence—likely combined with the frustration that he wished he had more hypothetical funds to utilize—brought a reaction from Joshua's mouth: 'Dad, this takes so much work!'

Within the number-flowing labor, Joshua expressed a cardinal truth: what is worthwhile to accomplish takes a great deal of craftsmanship and discipline. While money matters and life organization might come naturally to some, for many people it is a process that takes a massive amount of determination and intentionality. We require a number of things to continue living responsibly into the next day: money, health, activity, nutrition, sleep, and so on. We have a limited amount of time to make each day count. While there are a number of items in life *outside* of our control, we do have an orbit of details that we *can* influence. Our choices about our life and its activities matter a great deal.

With that being said, what sort of choices do we make? In addition, why do these choices matter? And what are some constructive, sensible attitudes and actions we can employ, because let's face it – this is the only life we get!

'What?': Defining Personal Stewardship

Think of personal stewardship as a mix of several meaningful items at once. Each of these is important in its own right. Also, no one really accomplishes excellence in all of these areas all the time. If you find that you are doing reasonably well in one of these categories but need significant improvement in the other two … well, hop in line with everyone else. It just proves you're human!

Productivity is the use of skill to accomplish things of significance. Notice I didn't say 'work' or 'family.' If we are connected to others (especially those who depend upon our labor for survival), then we cannot neglect our workforce obligations. And we should never become workaholics at the expense of our human relationships. The proper balance must be struck. But throughout the Bible, we see God placing a high value on human productivity. Proverbs 22:29 declares, 'Do you see a man skillful in his work? He will stand before kings; he will not stand before obscure men.' St Paul tells the Christians in Colosse that '[w]hatever you do, work heartily, as for the Lord' (Col. 3:23). And productivity is directly related to the provision for oneself and one's family. Paul says as much to the Thessalonicans when he reminds them that 'if anyone is not willing to work, let him not eat' (2 Thess. 3:10).

Wealth is your financial level and stability. It also reflects your attitudes toward money and how it should be used. Wealth is a tool. It is not the end goal in itself, but it is something used for something else. But as part of God's provision for us, wealth can be a blessing. Chieftains like Abraham[1] and landowner-merchants like Boaz[2] possessed considerable amounts of wealth and assets that benefited themselves, their families, and their wider communities.

A *healthy lifestyle* is also of great importance. We are physical beings; we have bodies, and we should care for and nourish those bodies insofar as we are able. Scripture reminds us that 'your body is a temple of the Holy Spirit within you ... glorify God in your body' (1 Cor. 6:19-20). Even when he is primarily talking about marriage, Paul sneaks in a side comment that 'no one ever hated his own flesh, but nourishes and cherishes it, just as Christ does the church' (Eph. 5:29). Several factors go into a healthy lifestyle of personal stewardship, but the key components are diet, exercise, and sleep.

Now that we've defined these components, why are they so critical in our embodied existence?

'So What?': Assessing Personal Stewardship

As with anything of value, to be <u>productive</u> takes *preparation*. Consider entering the workforce. If you wish to manage an information security business, you will need to (a) learn

---

1. See Genesis 12-25 for Abraham. He wouldn't have been able to shell out for a plot of land in Genesis 23 unless he had a measure of wealth.

2. See the book of Ruth. Boaz is not only well-to-do but is also highly respected, and one can see that part of the reason for this respect and honor was how he cared for the poor, widows, and other people on the margins of society.

quite a bit about computers and data systems and (b) develop considerable people skills so you can train and treat your fellow workers well. Being a teacher requires mastery of a subject matter, like science, and fostering patience toward students of all kinds. To be a counselor or marriage therapist, you must learn psychology and have both compassion and internal durability for the life stories of others. The same goes for starting a family if you want to be a productive parent. You must prepare by (a) knowing and loving more deeply the person you desire to marry, (b) sacrificing your needs for the needs of others, and (c) be ready to exhibit discipline and love toward your children.

Wealth also takes preparation. One of the biblical and common-sense particulars about wealth is that it takes disciplined effort. The virtuous wife of Proverbs 31 calculates a strategic plan, has knowledge about sales, and knows how to invest money and what to buy. But we should never let go of the fact that wealth is a tool. Money is not the end goal, but a portal toward proper provision. Think of wealth as financial food. To have food within your house is good (that certainly rates better than having an empty refrigerator), but if you never use it, you'll starve; additionally, if you overeat in large quantities or if you consume unhealthy amounts of junk, your life will not be as high of quality as it could be. Similarly, piling up a bank account might seem impressive, but you need practical wisdom to use money properly so that you might have a more flourishing existence.

A *healthy lifestyle* is also critical because if you are functioning physically as well as you can, then your productivity and provision have a greater chance of flourishing. Diet can be a sticking point for many people because the conversation can revolve around what foods you must avoid. But biblically, there are many positive statements about our food and drink. Psalm 104:14-15 speak highly of this, praising God for His provision:

'You cause the grass to grow for the livestock and plants for man to cultivate, that he may bring forth food from the earth and wine to gladden the heart of man, oil to make his face shine and bread to strengthen man's heart.' Very little biblical detail is given about the need for exercise. Granted, there weren't any Gold's Gyms open in ancient Israel, but given the robust workload for many in biblical times, one can surmise many tasks took a fair level of physical fitness! And we also need time to recharge and rest. That is one reason why God gave us the Sabbath day,[3] but even the rest and sleep He gives us is a profitable gift from Him (Ps. 127:2).

'Now What?': Applying Personal Stewardship

Given the importance of personal care, what are some strategies we can employ in the care of our bodies and lives? This is by no means an exhaustive list, nor is what follows a claim that I execute the following ideas in flawless fashion. Think of them as some suggestions and you can add more specific applications to them depending on your personal journey.

When it comes to productivity, I cannot stress enough that you let go of any idea that you'll discover your 'dream job' in your younger years. My students often speak about the careers (and bank accounts) they hope to have right out of their university years. Granted, some will find their desire and their career are an exact match, but this may not be the case for everyone. What you will likely discover is that the career you start with is not where you will finish. You may likely have a 'starter position' for three or four years and acquire some skills and habits that lead to another position with a different organization, after which you spend a few years there and then move to another group and tackle different tasks.

---

3. Exodus 20:9-10 and Exodus 31:15.

Part of being a productive person means having the willingness to be a humble learner, someone who listens well, follows directions, and develops practices and attitudes that may play well in the next chapter of your vocation.

Also, be willing to do anything. In the early days of my teaching career, I worked different jobs during the summer holidays. One summer, I boxed fire extinguishers on an assembly line; the next summer, I loaded furniture for delivery and helped with inventory; the following three summers, I delivered pizzas for Domino's! One thing that stood out to me was how often my superiors had their eyes on people who dove in and did their best. At the fire extinguisher factory, the manager asked if I would be willing to be the assistant manager! The next summer, the furniture store manager offered me a position in sales! Granted, my passion was teaching, so I declined both offers, but it was heartening to hear those men say what they did. If you bring a productive attitude to any activity, you might open up doors and expand options that God might be bringing your way. You never know.

Your wealth will also be a living advertisement to others about what is truly important to you. While not everyone reading this will have the same income level, you can have a proper strategy toward the wealth you have. The first step is to have a reasonable sense of what you can afford, and so adjust your expectations to the reality that is your financial accounts. In short, budget what you have. Set reasonable goals each month for what you can spend money on. This is especially critical for families, as there are more people affected by decisions on saving and spending. If your take-home income is seven thousand dollars per month, don't consistently spend ten thousand dollars per month. It makes no sense to be habitually spending money you don't have (let alone the negative impact to your credit standing). Take time to look at your spending habits every month, whether you tally it in a checkbook register or track your accounts online.

Note especially your discretionary spending. What things are eating up a significant amount of your income? Do you need to spend the money you have in each of these areas? How essential are some of the things on which you expend your funds? Could you get by with eliminating some items from your 'needs matrix'?[4]

And remember that acquiring wealth is only part of the goal. You never know what the future might bring, so it makes all the sense in the world, in whatever way you can, to put amounts aside for later use for yourself or others. And recall that ultimately, God owns everything (yes, even your salary is a gift from God), and so we should be in the habit of giving to our Redeemer and to others in need. When it comes to personal wealth, the mantra of former evangelist John Wesley is a helpful reminder: 'Make as much as you can, save as much as you can, give as much as you can.'

Practical matters of diet, exercise, and rest extend well beyond the few suggestions I could make here. The specific details of one's diet are not rigorously laid down as part of a mandatory Biblical regimen.[5] Also, depending if you live in Philadelphia, Pennsylvania or Athens, Greece or Kigali, Rwanda

---

4. Consider the accessibility of television channels. Some families might spend a small fortune on cable TV channels along with different tiers of sports and movie programming. I'd ask how much Showtime or HBO can one watch during their waking hours? Think about what you actually *need* and allow that to dictate your spending habits. This is where possibilities like Sling TV can give people more manageable options.

5. While there are a number of dietary laws for God's people in the Old Testament, it is my conviction that—as the people of God are now the Church and not national Israel—the dietary laws of that era are no longer required for people to follow. Maybe you find a more kosher diet is good for you, and that can be helpful. I just don't see that it's *mandated* for us.

or Ulaanbaatar, Mongolia, your food choices and desires will be largely determined by that culture. Some diets are more bread-oriented, some rely on fish, some more on vegetables, and so on. The key principle is to eat enough without overdoing it, and take in what will nourish you to be productive.

Exercise is an area where many (myself included) can improve. In some places, the physical labor done throughout the day can serve as enough exercise. Some might do better to join a health club that has an array of exercise equipment. The main ideas are *consistency and balance.* God has created us as physical beings, so some level of fitness for our bodies is most appropriate. But we should not overdo things. We can idolize our bodies and peak fitness so much that we over-train ourselves to the neglect of any balance to the rest of our lifestyle.

Finally, you are not intended to be in constant motion. As God prescribed a Sabbath day for His people to enjoy for rest each week, you must discipline your body and mind to 'Sabbath itself' daily. Get the proper sleep and down time you can muster. This is essential for personal productivity, but it also reminds us of something else: God is in control of life, and we are not. When we willfully shut down our mind and lie down in our beds, we are entering a holy space. We are admitting to God, 'You are sovereign. You'll watch over me when I sleep. I don't have to be in motion acting like things all depend on me. God, I trust you to handle all the details of my life.' Rest is a way to remind yourself of that most critical of truths: there is a sovereign, loving, good God, and you are not Him.

For Your Consideration

- Do you think it's more important to be a productive person or a wealthy person? How does a healthy lifestyle play into either of those categories?

- The author says, 'But we should never let go of the fact that wealth is a tool. Money is not the end goal, but a portal toward proper provision.' What happens when acquiring money becomes the main purpose rather than being a tool for provision? How does 1 Timothy 6:6-10 provide a good corrective here?

- The author also says, 'Your wealth will also be a living advertisement to others about what is truly important to you.' Think about what you consistently spend money (and time) on. What does this reveal about your priorities and what kind of person you might be? Are there changes you need to make?

18

Workforce Stewardship (Business Integrity)

ALTHOUGH I've spent the majority of my adult years as a teacher, I've had the privilege of laboring in many different positions over the years. Such opportunities include the following: bagger at a local grocery store, food preparer at Taco Bell, summer sales representative for Nabisco, vacuuming for a home cleaning company, sales associate at an athletic clothing store in a mall, volunteer firefighter when I was in college, janitor at a hospital, window washer for a private company, and then (as mentioned in the previous chapter) assembly line worker for a fire extinguisher factory, associate in a furniture store, and a driver for Domino's Pizza. If you count the school years I spent coaching American football, soccer, and baseball, we can add even more to my resume.

Some of these jobs were brief, almost all of them part-time. But every one of them was important to me. I was able to gain skills, hone instincts, and deepen an empathy for other people. Every job you hold, every company you work for, and every detail you accomplish is significant.

It's not because of what your salary might be, by the way. Nor does this significance get measured in terms of how far within a company you may be promoted. It's because God values all work that truly honors Him.

'What?': The Blessing of Work

In an episode of *The Simpsons* from years ago, Bart explodes with rage over being underpaid for several hours of hard, physical labor for an elderly lady. As the anger spills over, he lashes out, 'I'm never working again! Work is for chumps!' His father Homer, blending his rare fatherly joy with his usual Simpson cluelessness, puts his arm around Bart and says, 'Son, I'm proud of you! I was twice your age before I figured that out!'

It's sad when anyone utters sentiments along those lines. Of course, it is true that earning a living can feel like difficult activity. Hardship can intermingle with our labor. After the incident known as the Fall into sin, God counters Adam and Eve's hollow excuses with an explanation of how their newly wrought rebellion will affect the remainder of humanity. He tells Adam specifically that 'cursed is the ground because of you; in pain you shall eat of it all the days of your life; thorns and thistles it shall bring forth for you; and you shall eat the plants of the field. By the sweat of your face you shall eat bread, till you return to the ground, for out of it you were taken; for you are dust, and to dust you shall return' (Gen. 3:17b-19).

However, keep several things in mind. God is in no way telling Adam that work will be a joyless enterprise from now on. Of course, Adam (and we) can find a great deal of delight in the places where we work. God is merely letting us know that our work endeavors can be marked by hardship. Our relationships with colleagues can show evidence of conflict and distrust. Corporations, organizations, and other business syndicates may aim for higher profit margins by any means necessary without any thought of decency and honesty. Our own limitations of energy and wisdom in accomplishing tasks can become painfully obvious. These are clear realities in the broken world we live in.

But this is a world that retains the goodness it bears from being created by God, no matter how deeply human sin might have vandalized its glory. Though human labor might be spoiled, it is a *worthy activity*. Work did not come about as a result of the Fall, so it is not 'for chumps' (no matter what Homer and Bart Simpson might believe). Genesis 2:15 demonstrates that work is a central focus of God's creation *before the Fall!* It tells us that '[t]he LORD God took the man and put him in the garden of Eden to work it and keep it.' Notice what this means.

'Took': Our work and labor is neither accidental nor haphazard. I believe God is using this example of Adam to show us what God does in every one of our good endeavors that can please Him. Your accomplishments are provided under the umbrella of God's sovereignty. Your life is under God's hand.

'Put him': God is intentional about the opportunities in front of you. Whether we believe our present vocation is long-term or short-term, whether or not we believe we are making the highest use of our talents and abilities, God is not in the business of making mistakes. Do you have a job where you might provide for yourself and others? Well, that's because God is determined that it be so.

'Garden of Eden': Not everyone has a job that is ideal (and not everyone has a job, so we should also have compassion for the unemployed), but to have a place, a location to labor is a good thing! The physical, material world is a good place to be, because God has made it good.

'Work it': Labor is to be done well. One's work should be marked by diligence, craftsmanship, and dedication. Whatever might be said about anyone, loafing on the job should not be in those descriptions.

'Keep it': Ultimately, this is not about you. You work so you might serve God and others, for the good of those around you and for the glory of the God who provides for you. Yes, we are producers, but we are primarily stewards. Our labor is a way of showing God that we do care to treat our spheres of influence the right way.

'So What?': The Essentials of Work

Therefore, if God has given us the chance to labor, and if work is an enterprise that is at the core of humanity before God's world was marked by sin, then being part of the workforce is an opportunity to be involved in what God is doing throughout His world. It means we implicitly believe that what God has called us to do has *value*. There must be dignity and worth attached to our efforts, and as we harness those efforts in ways that produce income for ourselves and goods and services for others, we need to think about how our work efforts reflect that.

I am never ashamed to admit that others can clarify this better than I can. In fact, one of my colleagues, Jonathan Horn, has been very helpful here. Jonathan teaches business, marketing, and entrepreneurship at the same school where I teach. I love conversing with Jonathan because he has the ability to see the big picture of how God's calling and our labor come together. With his eye on the concept of value, Jonathan teaches how businesses and workers can position themselves to follow God's empowering call so that the value that results from our efforts can help people to flourish in their environment.[1]

---

1. Jonathan has created several sites for Westminster Christian Academy's business & communications department, where he serves as chairman. This information is largely drawn from their Company800 site at https://sites.google.com/a/wcastl.org/the-westminster-school-of-business-and-communication/introductiontobusiness/ createconnectcapture, but there's a LOT of good stuff throughout Jonathan's entire online presence through Company800.

First, businesses should have a proper vision of *creating value*. As God has made us to reflect Him in a culture-shaping capacity, it's altogether proper for businesses and corporations to deliver valuable goods and services to others. These goods and services must either (1) create a positive and helpful experience for the consumer or (2) reduce or eliminate hardship. For instance, companies like Harry's or Dollar Shave Club make quality shaving and grooming products for men.[2] The food delivery services GrubHub and DoorDash have redefined how many people eat by providing an on-demand approach to getting meals from favorite restaurants.[3] And of course, in a number of cases, the offer of a service prevents chaos and disorder. My friend Chris oversees product and research and development teams for a software company that manages document imaging, records management, and information protection. Through his company's work, many businesses can breathe more easily that their digital records and information are kept safe. In these (and other) scenarios, workplaces seek to produce something of critical requirement to consumers that the consumers aren't able to manufacture as well for themselves. In short, they are filling an essential need.

Secondly, there is the matter of *connecting value*. This is the process through which the company delivers the product to the consumer. This is actually more complex than it sounds. To connect value to others, a business must communicate its vision and product clearly; the company must treasure their consumer highly enough to make them aware of what they receive, often reinforced by how the goods or service are marketed. Interestingly enough, this doesn't require piles of

---

2. https://observer.com/2016/08/harrys-gillette-dollar-shave-club/. Full disclosure: I happen to like Harry's myself.

3. https://www.ridester.com/doordash-vs-grubhub/

money going to television advertisements or slick marketing campaigns. The Arizona Beverage Company, known for their Arnold Palmer lemonade-iced tea blend and a host of other drinks, relies on the recognition of their unique cans and social media outreach as marketing enough, and drinkers know they are getting a quality product. Aside from marketing techniques, consumers are looking for sales methods marked by integrity (in short, what you promise is what you get) and that a continued relationship will be beneficial. One reason why Chick-Fil-A fast food restaurants are highly successful derives from the quality of its food and the dignity with which sales help treats each customer.[4]

Lastly, the business must *capture value*. Don't be cynical and say, 'Oh, yeah, that's just because they need to feed their families.' Well, don't we all? Nothing wrong with that. Yes, we come to the point where the business takes in money in exchange for the goods or services provided. There is the question of *how much*. This goes beyond simplistic arithmetic. Yes, there's the matter of the sale price plus the cost of production plus the cost of delivery, but the business needs to calculate profit above this in order to figure wages for their employees. There are also other factors like what prices your competitor(s) might charge for the same product; do you make your goods slightly cheaper to boost sales or do you offer the same or slightly higher prices with better customer service? Or might you find methods of production that can be less pricey so that you can offer a product at a lower price?

To return to the Arizona Beverage Company, they discovered they could decrease the amount of aluminum in their cans by 40 per cent and still make fifteen thousand cans per minute,

---

4. https://www.sas.com/en_us/insights/articles/marketing/a-lesson-in-customer-service-from-chick-fil-a.html

thus keeping the price for a 23-ounce can of iced tea at less than an American dollar! And they still brought in $6.1 **billion** in revenue in 2018![5] I know money can sound like a crass subject to some, but businesses need to capture value *because if they don't, then they cannot continue to provide for the flourishing of other human beings through their work.* Far from being a dirty thing, money is a tool that can provide for the good of others in increasing capacity.

'Now What?': The Ingredients of Work

Workforce stewardship is highly important because so much of the human race enters the business world, whether for larger corporations or small businesses. What are some practical applications that we can take from all this?

First of all, I need to address the issue that, even though it is important for one's faith to connect with their work experience, there are some occupations in which that is impossible and therefore followers of Jesus should avoid these areas. I think we can agree on a number of those (drug dealing, prostitution, pornography, etc.). Also, when you find yourself considering occupations and vocations, be extremely wise if offered a position in a line of work that would make your faith highly difficult to live out. Any place that would require or strongly urge you to compromise on living out the gospel and the good life in Christ is a place where you are flirting with danger.

Secondly, there are many places where followers of Jesus need to be. Some of my former students have expressed that they need to go into Christian ministry to be highly used by God in their adult years. They need to be in a Christian vocation, not a secular one, they tell me. Many times, I've had to talk them

---

5. https://www.marketwatch.com/story/how-99-cent-cans-of-arizona-iced-tea-became-cheaper-than-bottled-water-2019-03-19

out of that because *if God has dignified human labor, there is no true sacred-secular split in the workplace.* God has blessed business and the marketplace of goods and services. Remember that when God created the world, which included humans who would be working (recall Adam was a farmer), God said all of it was 'very good.' Keep all your options open.

Another item: Your words and your actions are your bond of trust. If you are a mechanic and the repairs are minimal, don't make up problems that aren't there. If the right action is to charge two hundred and fifty dollars to get a Chevrolet in running condition, don't hit the customer with a four-hundred-dollar bill. Perhaps you are involved in mortgage lending for new homebuyers. You may not be able to promise exact details on the terms of a loan, but you can give a range of what buyers might be able to expect. Are you in the medical field? Don't overcharge patients. Are you a teacher? Be clear with students about your expectations.

One other truth I would urge you to apply is this: The people to whom you will be selling products to are not to be viewed merely as potential money-tossers. They are people with families, folks trying to live to the next paycheck, individuals made in God's image and therefore wrapped with all the dignity that can possibly be given to them. Remember, David proclaims in Psalm 8 that we are made 'a little lower than the angels', so that says something about the value of those with whom we interact when making sales and offers and negotiations. A colleague of mine told me that he enjoys 'investing in people.' That language is easy to slip into, but to use economic vocabulary to describe people as a product is not God-honoring. Make customers feel like they're the only people in the room. If you want your customers to return, or recommend your company to five of their friends, treat them like the near-angel the Bible claims they are.

In short, others do not exist primarily to make you wealthier; you exist to make the world around you more and more like God's dream for this world is coming true. And that is where business integrity truly begins.

For Your Consideration

- Observe how the author explains the elements of Genesis 2:15. What words and truths now take on a new meaning for you? Does seeing how God views human workmanship change your view about your choice of labor?

- If you are thinking of going into the business world (or are already there), what is your assessment of Jonathan Horn's categories of <u>creating</u>, <u>connecting</u>, and <u>capturing</u> value? Which of those categories particularly excites you? In what ways can you display a godly perspective in those areas?

- The author says that '*if God has dignified human labor, there is no true sacred-secular split in the workplace.*' Do you agree or disagree, and why? And if that statement is true, what implications does it have for the way we work?

19
Environmental Stewardship

MY daughter goes to a local fitness center for thrice-weekly workouts. The facility is somewhat stream-lined and narrow (some might say cramped), so when I go there to pick her up at the end of the workout, I take a seat on a steel chair next to a waste can. Recently, the owner of the center placed a sign on the waste can to head off a developing problem. It simply said, 'Put your empty plastic water bottles in the recycling can at the back, or you'll have to do twenty-five squat thrusts!'

I don't know if they've had problems with people chucking their plastic in the trash since then, but I think the wisdom on that sign displays a two-fold truth. One, we need to take care of our surroundings. Two, there are consequences if we don't. And those consequences are more staggering than a set number of squat thrusts.

'What?': The Planetary Summons

Taking care of the world around us in a way that—as a former colleague of mine once said—thinks globally and acts locally is a privilege and duty that God Himself puts in the hands of human beings from the very beginning. From the beginning of the Bible, we see majestic evidence that we live in a beautiful art gallery crafted and painted by God. The entire swath of planet Earth is, in the words of the Victorian poet and priest Gerard Manley Hopkins, 'charged with the grandeur of God.'

Not only is the universe an imprint of God's creativity and joy, but the fact that it is a *physical* entity gives the Lord a great deal of happiness. In consistent yet escalating fashion, He declares His work at each stage of creation as 'good', until He surveys everything He made, giving the entire world the capstone declaration of 'very good' (Gen. 1:4, 10, 12, 18, 21, 25, 31). Note what this means: There should be no divide in our view that the spiritual realm is holy and the physical world is not.[1] The physical world is *good*; it is a blessing that we can see, smell, touch, and taste *stuff*. And when human history is over, we do not float up from here into a spiritual form in the clouds. The new heavens and new earth *come down here* (Rev. 21:1-5) and everything about our world is not destroyed but *renewed*. We will have renewed *bodies* living in a renewed *physical environment*.

An additional element of environmental stewardship is that God has placed the baton of *dominion* in our hands. This comes from being made in God's image and likeness[2] (Gen. 1:26-28). We are commanded to reproduce on the earth, to subdue the earth, and to have dominion over the animal kingdom. This

---

1. When Christians start thinking in this two-story divide, they have little in common with the Bible and more in common with ancient Gnosticism, a sect that played havoc with early Christianity. Gnostics were all over the map on many issues, but one key tendency was that they believed the spirit world was good and the material world was evil, a teaching located nowhere in the Bible. For more information on the dangers of Gnosticism, see Irenaus' *Against Heresies* or chapter 2 of Justin Holcomb's *Know the Heretics* (Zondervan, 2014).

2. 'Made in God's image' can be one of those phrases that flies around conversations like a rugby ball over a Welsh pitch. So many people use those words without defining what they mean. Take it for what it's worth, but I tend to say that being made in God's image means we *reflect* God's nature and characteristics (in obviously limited fashion) and *represent* God on earth as His appointed governors.

throws light on two realities. First, we are participating as movers and shakers who make an impact on the world around us. God has left humans in charge, and we have a shaping role in how we unearth the capabilities and riches of this planet.

Secondly, *to subdue* does not mean to *subjugate*, and *dominion* does not mean *domination.* John Calvin lays this out in his warm yet precise style when he commented on Genesis 2 years ago when he said that '*this economy, and this diligence, with respect to those good things which God has given us to enjoy, may flourish among us; let everyone regard himself as the steward of God in all things which he possesses. Then he will neither conduct himself dissolutely, nor corrupt by abuse those things which God requires to be preserved.*'[3] In other words, we refuse to do nothing, and yet we don't ravage the earth for selfish measure.

All of these truths lead us to this understanding: The earth is not God, but it is a beautiful gift from God. To paraphrase one Christian writer, we do not worship nature when we live out God's call to creation care.[4] God rules the universe; we do not. However, God expects us to take seriously how we nurture what He endows us. And the consequences can be severe. In Revelation 11:18, we peek through the window of the future, when God will visit His wrath on those who seek to wipe out both His people *and* His creation. The twenty-four elders in heaven literally praise God 'for destroying the destroyers of the earth.'

'So What?': Why It Matters

Quick confession: I'm not a scientist (You likely guessed that already). I am not one who can wade easily through the data and arguments for and against global warming, for example. If

---

3. From Calvin's comments on Genesis 2:15.

4. See Tony Campolo's *How to Rescue the Earth Without Worshiping Nature* (Thomas Nelson, 1992).

you want specifics on those details, they are all over the Internet and in respected publications. I'm merely trying to answer the question 'Why should we care?'

First of all, this is your home. For eternity. As said before, the new heavens and new earth are coming down here. By virtue of the fact you are living here, you should seek to keep your home looking nice and care about the life others can enjoy on this journey. Please do not say, 'Yes, but if the world will be renewed anyway, then why does it matter if we trash it now?' The life of any human being—much more so the Christian believer—should be one of narrowing what I call the *shalom deficit* in this world: taking what is broken and disjointed and warped and making it as whole and useful as possible.

In this way—and I'm talking to followers of Jesus here—you are practically following your Master as you should. In several places in the New Testament, the Apostle Paul aligns Adam with Jesus Christ – the first human with the Savior.[5] Recall that when God entrusted dominion to humanity, He was speaking to Adam, the first man. Adam is given responsibility to exercise proper dominion. Yes, he failed by sinning and we follow along in his moral wreckage, but that didn't excuse him from his (and our) earthly responsibilities. Then Jesus, the second Adam, arrives on the scene. Not only does He turn back the great ruin of sin through His death and resurrection, but He takes on the role of a servant and aligns Himself with us in our humanity. If we are followers of Jesus, then shouldn't our lives be those of service? And if we live that way, isn't part of our Christ-like action to continue to undertake responsibility for God's creation?

Another opportunity Christians have in taking environmental stewardship seriously is that it can be a chance for others to see who God is. Unleashing the beauty of the earth and seeking

---

5. Especially in Romans 5.

a better environment can witness to God's power and nature. In Romans 1, the Apostle Paul notes that God's qualities and amazing characteristics are always on display through what He's crafted around us. Making sure people can maintain those glimpses might be one of the ways others can discover God so they might love and submit to Him.

There are other questions to consider: How do we make the earth properly inhabitable for a worldwide population that has climbed past seven billion?[6] Advocates, politicians, businesses, and scientists have to balance competing human needs. For instance, shelter is a basic human need, so it makes sense that we should endeavor that adequate housing exists. Business can demand physical buildings for commercial enterprises. However, if the construction of certain housing developments or business complexes overhauls the ecosystem to the degree that significantly hamstrings the flourishing of humanity, what then? If a two hundred home subdivision wipes out flora and fauna—or say a prevalence of bees or other critical insects— that hugely impact our lives, could that be a problem?

There is another point to consider: flipping things around where people *exclusively* pursue alternative forms of energy and cut out *existing* methods is not the wisest option. Should we try to develop opportunities in wind and solar power? Yes, by all means. Having more forms of energy development gives societies more choice in how to provide for their populations. Yet this doesn't mean we have to shut down oil drilling and fossil fuels. Those industries generate electricity, heating, and mobility at rates that are much more cost-effective compared to other methods. Many of the things we take for granted—

---

6. The population of Earth was two billion in 1930. Think about that. It took from the start of time to 1930 to get up to two billion people on the planet. We've added five billion more in less than ninety years since.

writing utensils, shirt buttons, shampoos, protective coating of furniture, trucking that transports goods you buy, and heating and cooling systems—are the result of the production of hydrocarbons from fossil fuels. It seems wisest to multiply energy producing options, rather than eliminating what already exists.[7]

That's just one example, but there can be many more. There are cases in which natural resources and people groups in need of those items can be unnecessarily separated. That's a problem that demands a solution. And I'm not prescribing if it should be solved by the government only or individuals only (although for efficiency of service and for personal compassion, I tend to default to individuals and private foundations), but the need of others should provoke empathy and action. For example, noting the lack of clean drinking water in east Africa, the Chris Long Foundation has built two dozen wells in Tanzania to bring this basic human need to the devastatingly poor.[8]

Yes, this seems like a daunting task when you consider the needs of the planet and its people. But if you ask the question, 'Is it worth it?', one can say 'To you or to God?'

'Now What?': Practical Ways to Help

Yes, you can contribute your money to organizations that assist in these areas, but there's no doubt that you can do little things every day that can make modest yet consistent impact for the good of the environment. We can think critically about how we use our own resources, like food. Think about how much you throw away, eh? Keep your leftovers for meals in the near

---

7. For a quick glance at this, read Andree Seu Peterson's brief piece, 'Gifts for Life', at https://world.wng.org/2019/05/gifts_for_life

8. See https://chrislongfoundation.org/initiatives/ and https://waterboys.org/ for more information.

future. Be judicious about the amount of food in your pantry or refrigerator. If you have trouble keeping track of what's fresh and what isn't, you can download the Freshbox application to help you organize what's available and what needs to be used in a hurry.[9]

Recycling is another way we all can contribute. At home or at work, make sure that whatever can be re-used gets recycled. Paper, bottles, cans – and be assertive in doing so. We attended a church once that made their worship bulletins out of post-consumer paper that had been recycled. Just another example.

Give thought to the use of energy in your home. You should provide for your needs but think about moderation. Our hot water heater recently fizzled out after a thirty-three-year existence, so we had to purchase another in a hurry (I don't like to be forced into cold-water-only experiences). We wanted one that would adequately heat our home, but we refused to go beyond the capacity needed to do the job. If your home is two thousand square feet, buy an item that will heat the home you have, not one for a home twice as large just so you can have hot water more quickly. Think about what appliances do the best work most efficiently, and pay attention to what is most ideal to do that job, whether it be powered by electricity or natural gas.

This can go beyond the individual level to larger organizations. One of the football clubs (that's *real* football, what Americans call soccer) that I follow is Forest Green Rovers FC, based in Nailsworth, England. This League Two club plays quite competitive football, but they are even more well known for being the world's first comprehensive eco-friendly sports franchise. At the New Lawn (the Rovers stadium), the groundskeepers, for example, use cow manure to condition the

---

9. https://greatist.com/health/freshbox-app-keep-track-of-food

playing surface in the off-season, while using grass cuttings for the same purpose through the playing schedule.[10] To provide 10 per cent of the energy at the New Lawn, the team installed solar panels,[11] which also power the 'mow-bot', a robot mower that cuts the grass on the pitch using GPS technology.[12] In addition, the team recycles rainwater, saves waste cooking oil at the food stands and turns it into biofuel,[13] and authorized the planting of a wildflower reserve outside the stadium, enhancing the presence of owls, bees, butterflies, and house martins, among other species.[14]

So, whether you are one person acting alone or part of a larger group, you have more power to exercise proper dominion of God's world than you might imagine. Don't worry about whether you are changing things rapidly; being faithful in moving the meter in the right direction is what matters ... both for the planet and for the God who created it.

For Your Consideration

- Why do you think a number of people—including a not-too-small number of Christian believers—act as if it's okay to subjugate and exploit nature rather than having honorable dominion over the earth?

- How does the fact that—if you are a follower of Jesus—you will be living on a renewed earth affect how you take care of your environmental surroundings now?

10. https://www.bbc.com/news/uk-england-gloucestershire-13776435

11. https://www.bbc.com/news/uk-england-gloucestershire-16022775

12. https://www.bbc.com/news/uk-england-gloucestershire-17791690

13. https://www.weforum.org/agenda/2018/12/this-is-the-worlds-greenest-football-club-and-youve-probably-never-even-heard-of-it/

14. https://www.gazetteseries.co.uk/sport/9860125.new-lawn-hot-spots-are-blooming-lovely/

- How might we contribute to economic well-being and provision while still maintaining a healthy respect for creation and preserving the environment? What are some concrete solutions you can imagine?

20

Social Stewardship (Migration Challenges and Opportunities)

STEWARDSHIP is not merely limited to personal resources, business ethics, or how we manage God's creation. A further application of stewardship comes in the proper way Christians advocate for and participate in issues of global migration. In recent years, population migration has morphed into a contentious and sometimes divisive issue. Immigration policy debates have boiled over in places such as the United States, the United Kingdom, France, Germany, Poland, Hungary, and other nations. Among the complicating factors to these conversations arise the twin questions of freedom and security. There is a range of reasons why migration occurs, but freedom happens to be a concern that floats to the top. Whether running away from the upheaval of armed conflict or persecution in one's homeland or possessing the desire to relocate to more promising economic chances, there is no doubt many migrants seek more personal opportunity than where they once dwelt. However, in a post-9/11 world, where the spectre of terrorism looms large and malcontent radicals probe the soft spots across international borders to wreak havoc, personal and national security is just as rightful a concern.

Please don't expect a definitive, clinching argument for *what* the official policy should be on global migration. I'm simply not intelligent enough to speak to that, plus different territories will necessarily have different needs and varied reactions to how they must police their borders. And given that people move around the world for a variety of reasons, no two migrant stories are exactly alike. What I think is important, from a Christian perspective of God's world, is to put forth some non-negotiables that followers of Jesus *should believe* on migration and *what they can do* for migrants. So, my aim is a biblical baseline that will result in practical ways you might involve yourself.

'What?': What Is This Phenomenon?

From 1990 to the present day, population movement around the globe has grown especially fluid and brisk. We are experiencing an unprecedented shift in foot traffic around the planet through migration. When we speak of an international migrant, we mean 'a person who is living in a country other than his or her country of birth.'[1] Whatever the individual reasons are for those leaving places behind, migrants tend to fall in either (or both) of two main categories:

Immigrants, for the sake of our discussion, are those who are moving from one nation to another for the primary purpose of expanded opportunities for the individual or a family group. Throughout history, there have been hardships that influence immigration, so that a calamity motivates people to seek happiness and improved circumstances elsewhere. The Irish potato famine of 1845 to 1849 brought on the death of one million citizens of Ireland while a million more emigrated from the

---

1. http://www.un.org/en/development/desa/population/migration/publications/ migrationreport/docs/MigrationReport2017_Highlights.pdf, p. 3. Hereafter, I'll refer to this as the 'UN Report'.

Emerald Isle, mostly to America.[2] Other times, increased possibilities do not arise from adversity but simply from a chance to better one's existing status. In Hong Kong, the United Arab Emirates, Singapore, Liechtenstein, and Luxembourg, immigrants make up at least 40 per cent of the population due to expansive business ventures and opportunities.[3]

Refugees are distinct from immigrants. Refugees migrate because they *must*, due to persecution, war, violence, or other threat of destruction.[4] Bosnians left their nation in the midst of the Balkan War of the 1990s; Syrian refugees have fled the 2011-onward civil war there for asylum in Europe; many Somalians seek peace and a new life away from the continued violence in their land that has raged for more than a quarter-century. Nearly 26 million refugees are scattered over the planet today.[5] While refugees might come from all economic classes of their former society, their displacement can often leave them destitute.

Whatever description a migrant might bear is one issue. What is truly amazing is that the speed and volume of migration has multiplied greatly over the past twenty years. Individual nations have seen their migrant populations increase many times over. From 1990 to 2017, the United Kingdom experienced a rise in their migrant number from 3.65 million to 8.84 million, which is an eighth of Britain's overall population. Germany's migrants went from a total of 5.94 million to 12.17 million in the same

---

2. See Christine Kinealy's *This Great Calamity* for an engaging overview of the crisis.

3. The Asian locations are particularly notable. While American cable news telecasts might paint a picture of immigration occurring primarily on American or European shores, in truth Asia adds more migrants than any other geographical region.

4. https://www.unrefugees.org/refugee-facts/what-is-a-refugee/

5. UN Report, p. 7.

span of time, representing one-seventh of all people living there. The United States likewise went from 19.68 million to 44.41 million. Other nations such as Australia, Turkey, Denmark, and Norway have seen similar percentage increases.[6]

Another staggering reality is the extent of how far migrants will go to their new locations. Half of all migrants live not only in a different country from the place of their birth, but on a different *continent* than where they previously dwelt. And where do they tend to go? Usually, it's to higher income nations where opportunity and social welfare chances are more plentiful and can offer the safety nets migrants require.[7]

While the expansion of migration is an international phenomenon, it occurs within the tremors of a post-9/11 world of intense global security issues. While it is true that some of the resistance to migration amongst some groups is the sad result of xenophobia, racism, and the perceived 'threat to Western culture', many are rightly anxious about the security needs of citizens of their own nation. Checking migrants at a border to certify they are no threat is an intricate task, but in a setting where terrorism and violence can go viral, the need for measures to keep a sovereign nation safe is a legitimate concern. One example of domestic terrorism in America is the 2013 Boston Marathon bombings. Dzhokhar and Tamerlan Tsarnev were born in Kyrgyzstan, immigrated to the United States on a tourist visa, became naturalized citizens while radicalized by al-Qaeda, and then carried out the bombings.[8] Increases

---

6. http://www.pewglobal.org/interactives/international-migrants-by-country/ Obviously, this is not the case everywhere. There are some notable nations that have a decrease of migrants. Among these countries are Poland, Estonia, and Brazil.

7. UN Report, p. 4.

8. https://www.nbcphiladelphia.com/news/national-international/Boston-Bombing-Suspects-are-Russian-Brothers-Officials-Say-203757531.html

in violent crime in some areas of Germany have been highly attributable to migrant clusters.[9] These are factors that keep a number of people greatly concerned.

Without a doubt, we must endeavor to keep our fellow citizens in any country safe from harm. How that safety is applied can vary from nation to nation. Some places will have rigorous background checks upon migrant arrival. Other places might advocate building border walls. Not everyone will agree on how to protect others, but these are conversations worth having.

Still, followers of Jesus should tackle this issue by other means than downloaded reports from the United Nations or the sensationalism of television news digests, whether it be Fox News, CNN, or the BBC. First, we who are Christians place ourselves under the sovereignty of God. He can protect us better than any national government or military unit can from any danger (although let's admit, we don't want those institutions shirking their responsibilities). Plus, if we believe God has revealed His desires for us in the Bible, then perhaps Scripture has a few things to say on how we should approach this topic.

'So What?': Why Does This Matter to Followers of Jesus?

We don't even get out of the first chapter of the first book of the Bible before God makes His views plain. Well before national borders would redefine the globe, the Lord has a word with the first humans: 'Be fruitful and multiply *and fill the earth* and subdue it …' (Gen. 1:28). The expansion of the human species over the entire earth is part of God's ultimate design, so we should not be surprised when this happens.

In fact, when humans are resistant to this call to 'fill the earth', God meets their defiance with a stiff counteraction. Genesis 11 gives us the story of the tower of Babel. Many

---

9. https://www.bbc.com/news/world-europe-42557828

people on earth wanted to congregate together and stay in one location, even building a tower to heaven. Many readers of this passage might focus on the building of the tower to the skies and say the people's problem is their pride at trying to act like God. I'm sure there is some of that, but look at what the text says: They are doing all this 'lest we be dispersed over the face of the whole earth.' And God's response is to discombobulate their communications into many languages and scatter them in varied groups over the known world. God was absolutely determined to get people on the move.

A number of individuals very dear to God and critical to God's sovereign plans are also forced to go across borders, to migrate to other lands. In Genesis 12, the LORD tells Abram (later known as Abraham) to '[g]o from your country and from your kindred and your father's house to the land that I will show you' (Gen. 12:1). Even Abraham willingly admits in this new land of Canaan that 'I am a sojourner and foreigner among you' (Gen. 23:4a) and yet the natives treated him like a prince! Abraham's grandson Jacob ended up taking his entire family to Egypt because a famine broke out in their own territory, and they were welcomed and received with great hospitality (Gen. 46:1-47:12). Years later, a woman named Ruth leaves her country of Moab and goes with her mother-in-law Naomi to the town of Bethlehem in Israel. There she meets a man named Boaz, gets married, and becomes known as the great-grandmother of King David. And since Jesus Christ was descended from David's line, it means that the Savior's family tree has migrant bloodlines in it. The Bible seems to be directing us toward celebrating this truth.[10]

---

10. I've pretty much put the whole book of Ruth in a nutshell through these few sentences. I'd encourage you to read the book of Ruth as it's much more exciting than I can make it in this book!

Speaking of Jesus, He had to migrate, as well! Realizing through a dream that wicked King Herod intended to kill the infant Christ, Joseph took his wife Mary and his son to Egypt in the dead of night. There they hid out until things were safe enough to return (Matt. 2:13-15). It is also worth noting that once Jesus' earthly ministry was complete, He gave a significant command to His followers to 'make disciples of all nations' (Matt. 28:18-20). His followers were to instruct and mentor new followers across ethnic, economic, and national borders. Yes, we can certainly go outward toward those who need to hear the good news of Jesus. But just as surely, we might find that others are flooding our direction, and we have gospel opportunities with a plethora of nations on our own doorstep.

Those are good, biblical reasons that demonstrate that God is a Father who loves children who are on the move, bumping around His creation and being part of a majestic connection of one culture with another. There are other common-sense reasons why migration can be a healthy venture. It can open people up to being more well-rounded, compassionate souls, to extend kindness and hospitality to those in desperate situations. We are given opportunities to see how we are cut from the same human cloth and require basic needs and justice. Needless to say, this reminder, too, comes straight from the Bible. In ancient Israel, God's people were to 'have the same rule for the sojourner and for the native' (Lev. 24:22) and migrants were to be given access to food (Lev. 23:22). Part of learning how to be a decent human being comes with how we treat those who come from places different from our own.

'Now What?': What Can I Do?

It's true, you're just one person. You might believe there are limits to what you can do for migrants. Perhaps you feel strongly you should be working in a practical way but you are unsure what that looks like. There's no reason to be ashamed of that. There are some groups who have made strides in coming alongside migrants to offer physical relief, friendship, and a God-honoring welcome to those who feel like strangers in a strange land. What follows are some examples.

For instance, several thousand refugees come to my present residence of St Louis, Missouri, each year. These people arrive with little, if any, sense of what to expect, which places can offer them a fresh start, and the relationships they enjoy are in a small circle of their fellow migrants. A couple of years ago, the Missouri Baptist Convention began the Good Neighbor Initiative. Noting the numbers of refugees arriving from Iraq, Syria, Somalia, Afghanistan, and the Congo, the MBC mobilized to connect these refugees with people who could help.

Noting that less than 15 per cent of refugees are ever befriended by an American family, the MBC made raising that number a primary goal. Individuals, families, and Bible study groups could register to be part of the ministry. They would be partnered with a refugee family and thus committed to visiting the family or neighbor, to pray for them regularly, and invite them over for meals or picnics and other celebrations. Volunteers who are particularly gifted in construction and craftsmanship connect with other charitable foundations to provide safe, clean, and affordable housing to refugee families. Whether or not the refugees are followers of Jesus at the time is not the issue, although if opportunities for conversation about the Christian faith arise, they can happen. The main idea is to give migrants a place to belong and friends whom they can trust, to offer acceptance and friendship. And in time, relationships can lead to richer communities.[11]

---

11. See http://mbcpathway.com/2016/08/09/st-louis-association-calls-equips-churches-to-love-refugees/ Also, the program is laid out in more detail at http://goodneighborstl.com/

Other migrants might desire to not only move to a new location, but also, in time, become citizens of that nation. Depending on the demands of the citizenship process, migrants might be overwhelmed by the maze of paperwork and certifications and require help to understand each step of the way. My denomination, the Anglican Church in North America, began an immigrant initiative to provide legal aid for migrants who need help navigating the American court system. Rather than allowing Nigerian, Burmese, Sudanese, and Chinese folks to fall prey to unlicensed workers who pose as being more helpful than they actually are, the ACNA has attorneys who come alongside migrants and offer them practical assistance, forging opportunity for continued relationships with these people groups. And in the providence of God, it has even led the way for the establishment of many new immigrant churches![12]

You might not have the time or connections to be involved in situations exactly like those, but chances are your opportunities might be closer than you think. Perhaps in your school you know of students whose original home was somewhere beyond your borders. Yes, they might have clothes on their backs and, yes, they are taking the same coursework as you. But what they might crave most of all is for someone to show an interest in their story.

What about the Bosnian girl who sits in front of you in your history class? Might her parents harbor some resentment about the Balkan War? Could they have some stories about how they barely escaped being massacred? Maybe these stories are bottled up inside her and she just wants someone to listen compassionately. What about that South Sudanese guy who watches the ultimate Frisbee game on the college quadrangle

12. http://www.anglicanchurch.net/index.php/main/anglican_immigrant_initiative/

with a great deal of interest? Why don't you invite him to join? To get together for a meal or coffee afterwards? (He might even talk with great gusto about escaping from South Sudan into Kenya, where the coffee was much bolder than the cup he holds in his hands.)

But you notice you can make a lot of these connections spontaneously. Don't worry about the specifics of what to say. Just be friendly and down-to-earth and see where it goes. You'll likely find you are more ready than you can imagine for such an undertaking, and perhaps through it you'll be blessed with new friends as well.

For Your Consideration

- Do you think the Bible should be used as a guide for a nation's government policy on immigration? Why or why not?

- Do you know someone who was born elsewhere and came to your country, either for a better life or to escape danger? What about their story can you appreciate and value?

- How would you characterize the Bible's view of migrants? Why is this stance so helpful in developing our own understanding of this issue?

21

The Last Word Matters

IDEAS matter. Life matters. Relationships matter. Stewardship matters.

I wouldn't have addressed these many issues in the preceding chapters if I didn't believe them to be part of essential conversations.

We need to live wisely. We should live proactively. We need to be prepared to engage the world. We must be thoughtful in how we engage others.

But the results of all that are out of our hands. The results are up to God.

A Biblical view of the world—which well-crafted common sense will uphold and confirm—gives you and others the grandest, most wonderful opportunity to experience the good life that God offers us. Jesus Christ was not willing to stay remote from our world, but rather He entered our existence. Living the life we failed to accomplish and dying the savage death we deserved for our rebellion, Jesus fulfilled every requirement we couldn't meet. And when you place your wholehearted trust in Christ—in His life, death, and resurrection on your behalf—you are not only delivered from your rebellious consequences, but you are empowered to live as a delivered soul.

But again, the results are up to God. In 1 Peter 3:15, the Apostle Peter reminds us to *'always be prepared to make a defense to anyone who asks you for a reason for the hope that is in you, yet do it with gentleness and respect.'* You might convince others of the good life. You may struggle with others. But God does not call you to smashing success. He calls you to be resolute and generous, bold and kind. God doesn't want you to brandish converts to your cause like they are marks off a bucket list; He wants your loving, consistent allegiance.

My college history professor and dear friend, the late Dr Louis Voskuil, was fond of making that point. He'd remind us students that if you climbed the corporate ladder into six- and seven-figure salaries, that's fine, but you don't *have to.* If you have a large family in a home that is the essence of comfort and warmth, that's fine, but you don't *have to.* If you discover a groundbreaking cure for debilitating diseases, that's fine, but you don't *have to.* And if you write the greatest novel or ascend to political might, that's fine, but you don't *have to.* And he'd always close his reminder with the words, **'All that God requires of you is that you be faithful, and the rest will take care of itself.'**

When it comes to the details of what I've shared in this book, the goal is no different. Engage with others. Speak truth. Converse clearly. Offer the good life with hope and compassion. Jesus will take care of the details of how your friends and acquaintances will understand. And you'll find He does that better than you could ever imagine.

Christian Focus Publications

Our mission statement –

STAYING FAITHFUL

In dependence upon God we seek to impact the world through literature faithful to His infallible Word, the Bible. Our aim is to ensure that the Lord Jesus Christ is presented as the only hope to obtain forgiveness of sin, live a useful life and look forward to heaven with Him.

Our books are published in four imprints:

CHRISTIAN
FOCUS

Popular works including biographies, commentaries, basic doctrine and Christian living.

CHRISTIAN
HERITAGE

Books representing some of the best material from the rich heritage of the church.

MENTOR

Books written at a level suitable for Bible College and seminary students, pastors, and other serious readers. The imprint includes commentaries, doctrinal studies, examination of current issues and church history.

CF4•K

Children's books for quality Bible teaching and for all age groups: Sunday school curriculum, puzzle and activity books; personal and family devotional titles, biographies and inspirational stories – because you are never too young to know Jesus!

Christian Focus Publications Ltd,
Geanies House, Fearn, Ross-shire,
IV20 1TW, Scotland, United Kingdom.
www.christianfocus.com